Coming After Oprah

Coming After Oprah:
Cultural Fallout in the Age of the TV Talk Show

Vicki Abt
and
Leonard Mustazza

Bowling Green State University Popular Press
Bowling Green, OH 43403

Copyright ©1997 Bowling Green State University Popular Press

Library of Congress Cataloging-in-Publication Data

Abt, Vicki, 1942-
    Coming after Oprah : cultural fallout in the age of the TV talk show /
Vicki Abt and Leonard Mustazza.
        p.   cm.
    Includes bibliographical references and index.
    ISBN 0-87972-751-9 (clothbound). -- ISBN 0-87972-752-7 (paperback)
    1. Talk shows--United States.   I. Mustazza, Leonard, 1952-   . II. Title.
PN1992.8.T3A28   1997
791.45'6--dc21   97-13986
                                                                      CIP

Cover design by Dumm Art

For Harold Abt and Andrea Abt Jones
—V.A.

For Anna, Christopher, and Joseph Mustazza
—L.M.

Contents

Acknowledgments

We would like to express our gratitude to a number of individuals who have helped us in the writing of this book. For their helpful comments on various drafts of the manuscript, our thanks go to Richard, Marci, and Allison Abt and Matthew Wolchock. Thanks, too, to Christopher Mustazza for his assistance in conducting research. We very much appreciate the help and support of our many colleagues at Penn State University's Abington College, particularly Margaret Bodkin, Nancy Crabb, Ellen Furman, Dinah Geiger, Margaret Hindley, Carol Julg, Ellen Knodt, Phyllis Martin, Mel Seesholtz, Jim Smith, and Jeannette Ullrich.

Abington, Pennsylvania

Introduction

Everyone's avocation in America is show business. . . .
Television captures the imagination more than anything else in
people's lives. The country is somehow held together by
celebrities. . . . Celebrity talk-show people. . . . It's this jungle
of junk. . . . Junk information. Junk misinformation. Half-
baked knowledge. Received opinion. . . . You aren't anybody
in America if you're not on TV. In short, you don't exist unless
you're on TV."

> —Buck Henry, screenwriter
> for the movie *To Die For* (1995)

When I got my first television set, I stopped caring so much
about personal relationships.

> —Andy Warhol, pop artist,
> quoted posthumously in *New York* (1995)

We started doing confrontational TV. . . . I believe it was
important to introduce these issues and face the truth of who
we were. . . . Instead, TV got stuck thriving on them, and for
the worst possible reasons—exploitation, voyeurism, and
entertainment.

> —Oprah Winfrey,
> "What We All Can Do to Change TV,"
> *TV Guide* (1995)

There is no such thing as bad publicity. . . . I'd rather be
abused than not noticed.

> —P. T. Barnum

2 Coming After Oprah

The talk show as a confrontational display of personal conflicts among everyday noncelebrities, plucked from often well-
deserved obscurity, entered our cultural consciousness in the mid-
1980s with the syndication of the still top-rated *Oprah Winfrey
Show*. Oprah's competitor in the Nielsen ratings, Sally Jessy
Raphael, used a similar format several years before and argues that
it was she who introduced the first "family feud" to the confrontational mix, while now-retired Phil Donahue is credited with having
been the first syndicated talk-show host to have made "audience
participation" an integral element of the genre. Be that as it may, it
was the huge success of Oprah's daily program that changed the
scene and brought about the age of the TV talk show.

As analysts of cultural trends and themes, we are struck by the
comparison between the quiz-show scandal of the 1950s and the
daily scandal of such "toxic talk." While the quiz shows ended
their run because of a behind-the-scenes "fix,"[1] the answers they
broadcast were nevertheless factually true and nonthreatening to
civil culture. We might argue that the premise of the old quiz
shows—that knowledge, let alone wisdom, could be reduced to
short "factual" answers—was basically flawed. Yet, they were still
broadcasting benign information about various subjects, even if
the facts conveyed bordered on sound-bite measurements of what
"intellectuals" knew in detail. By contrast, despite occasional
reports of a ringer, or obviously fraudulent guest, the deceptive
premise of the contemporary talk show is far less innocent and
much more dangerously problematic than an obvious "fix." The
central problem is surely the inappropriate juxtaposition of sala-
cious anecdotes and emotional reactions by guests with a seemingly innocent, therapeutic, and helpful earnestness on the part of
hosts, studio audiences, and invited "experts" conventionally
reserved for much more private settings.

During the fall of 1991, Vicki Abt carried out a content analysis of three of the most popular talk shows at the time.[2] The result
was Abt and Seesholtz's "The Shameless World of Phil, Sally and
Oprah: Television Talk Shows and the Deconstruction of Society,"
which even before its publication in 1994, triggered the controversy that led to Vicki Abt's two-day appearance on *The Oprah
Winfrey Show* at the start of the 1994-1995 television season.

While defending the genre and herself against the study's conclusions, Oprah subsequently changed her show's focus, and the media began covering the issue widely.[3] Since that time, other voices of discontent from the right and the left have been heard, though not always the most unbiased of voices. Predictably—and ironically, given the conservatives' part in deregulating commercial television and arguing against public funds for public-broadcasting alternatives—Empower America's Bill Bennett and other politicians joined the attack on talk shows as part of their shotgun criticism of popular culture in general. However, few if any of these seriously criticize the commercial interests behind the media's message. Instead they confine their proposed "solutions" to homilies like "Just Say No" to the programs, or they put the onus on families to control their children's consumption of such toxins flooding the market.

After eight seasons of being the "Queen of Trash," Oprah Winfrey herself joined the rising tide against the genre that she created, recently lamenting the explosion in copycat talk shows that encourage people to brag about their irresponsible behaviors. Of course, this public change of heart after the damage has been done is really quite in keeping with talk-show formats and the electronic "confessional" in general. Nevertheless, she is perhaps the only popular talk-show host to have kept her word by radically overhauling her program, and *Oprah* is now surely the best of the genre. Others have made only cosmetic modifications in their format, promising things like "after care" programs or featuring half-minute "bulletins" on former guests or briefly describing at the end of a broadcast what happened to guests on a show. Still others have become even more cynical, concluding their shows with a minute or so of pontificating speech rejecting the guests and their behavior—after the same guests had been encouraged to carry on for the proceedings just aired.

In the four years since this study began, Abt has had the opportunity to go behind the scenes and to talk to producers, hosts, guests, and studio audiences. Most criticism of the genre is simply dismissed in on-air debates as "elitist." During many television and radio interviews, she has attempted to focus public discussion on issues beyond the interests of specific talk show "victims" unhappy with their appearances or of the "fake" guest or the highly publicized murder related to a guest appearance on one such talk show. Nevertheless, people remain fascinated by the individual players. Few question the shows' underlying distortions; fewer still discuss the shows in terms of the commercial empires behind their production or their relationship, despite headline-making announcements of media mergers, to the radical changes in enabling federal legislation. Interviewers and listeners who call in often ask whether the "guests" are actors or are paid participants. (Most are not professional actors, but that doesn't mean they aren't "acting," and those who are paid get so little that the motivation cannot largely be attributed to money.) Surprisingly few former guests have brought legal action against the shows. Among the handful of such known cases, a Pennsylvania woman has filed suit against the now-defunct *Charles Perez Show* (Daily v. Perez, et al., Case #95-6075) claiming that, after she refused to appear on the show with her sister to discuss their sex lives, the show's producers hired an actress to play her part opposite the real-life sister (Slobodzian B2). Abt herself was involved as an expert witness in a case brought against Geraldo Rivera and his syndicator, Tribune. After a judge excluded Mr. Rivera from the suit on technical grounds, the case was settled out of court.

But these cases are anomalies. In fact, the producers have more volunteers and satisfied former guests than they know what to do with. In 1995 Jerry Springer, for instance, told *Entertainment Weekly* that his show, then in its fifth season, received 3,000 calls a day from people wanting to tell their stories. He added that "Talk shows will never be in trouble because of the subject matter. The more controversial, the bigger the shows get" (Jacobs 35). Indeed, the talk shows are more in danger of running out of "shocking" topics than potential guests. The producers' arguments—"They have a story to tell" or "We're just giving audiences what they want" or "I only work here"—fail to deal with personal responsibility, the deceptive nature of the entire proceedings, and the dangerous implications of this kind of entertainment. Unfortunately, despite much criticism (which often turns out to be superficial hype), television talk shows proliferated, their content making the 1991 shows far less preposterous by comparison. *The Jerry*

Springer Show, for example, was one of the few nationally syndicated talk shows that saw a rise in its 1995 Nielsen ratings (Seplow, "Seduced" 14) despite the fact that it is generally considered
among the worst in terms of outrageous disclosures. All of this
suggests that if we think the talk show is in imminent danger of
extinction, we are mistaken. In this particular war, it is the worst of
programs that will most likely survive the glut on the television
market, and a jaded public will increasingly abandon those that are
less shocking. This book is our attempt to explain the forces that
contributed to their creation, transformation, and appeal in the last
decades of twentieth-century America.

According to a PBS documentary underwritten and distrib-
uted by the University of Notre Dame in which Abt was interviewed along with Phil Donahue and several media analysts, in
1985 there were fourteen hours of soap operas on daytime television and only four hours of talk shows. In 1995, by contrast, there
were fewer than ten hours of soap-opera programming and more
than twenty talk shows. Millions of people obviously enjoy this
new-age version of the game show as much as they enjoy soap
operas, perhaps more, and that fact ought to be disturbing. It is
unsettling, to say the least, that people's problems have become
America's entertainment. Despite attacks by politicians, evidence
of increasing unease among advertisers in the face of rising criticism, and a general ratings decline since 1990-1991—the talk
shows' most popular period—they generally continue to dominate
daytime television.

Over the years the topics, format, and talk have become
increasingly shameless, with the notable exceptions of Oprah's
new format and the recent variants of the pre-Oprah celebrity-
interview program (e.g., *The Rosie O'Donnell Show*). New shows
continue to be produced and marketed as revenues in general
climb. In 1993 (not Oprah's best ratings year), for instance, her
syndicator, King World, disclosed revenues of approximately $424
million, 39% or about $165 million of which was attributed to her
show. *The Wall Street Journal* reports that Philip Morris spent an
estimated $4.42 million from January 1 through August 31, 1995,
advertising on her top-rated show (Beatty B10). The same article,
nevertheless, cites Nielsen research data showing that ratings for

all talk shows actually fell to a weighted average of 3.5% of all TV homes in 1994-1995 from 4.3% in 1990-1991. The percentage among teen viewers, however, grew slightly in the same period, and the number of shows shot up from nine to twenty. Even the well-publicized March 1995 murder of a guest after taping a segment of *The Jenny Jones Show* earlier that same month was not the talk shows' death knell.

Amid the recent wave of media mergers these programs still promise large profits. In fact, the mergers, which will leave far fewer media competitors in the marketplace, look forward to the perfect marriage between the message and the media as new and inexpensively produced shows help finance some very expensive corporate acquisitions, further contributing to the "dumbing down"[4] of American audiences. Most recently, the 1996 Telecommunications Act has essentially deregulated the $700 billion industry that produces talk shows, and American culture may never quite recover.

Despite 1995-1996's flurry of "new" talk shows, however, there have been signs that the decade of toxic talk is gradually coming to an end. Given some sustained political pressure, advertisers' unease, and the general decline in viewer percentages, we have reason to believe that talk shows face an uncertain long-range future. Moreover, there appears to be some erosion in viewer interest, but whether talk shows will decline in popularity due to the saturation of the market, the possibility that audiences have become increasingly inured to such talk, or on the other hand, increasingly critical of them is an open question.

The last of these items is perhaps the most telling and ironic. Some talk-show hosts, in a self-serving effort to ease criticism, are themselves doing an about-face and calling for a "kinder, gentler" talk-show scene. But such self-conscious attempts to disarm critics often lead to the ludicrous display of a Jerry Springer, who at the close of one show, sanctimoniously exhorted his viewers to behave better than his guests. On another program Jerry Springer argued that he believes in the First Amendment and therefore never rejects people from appearing on his show "just because I might not agree with them." This claim came at the end of a particularly ugly tirade by a racist anti-Semite on a May 1996 segment showcasing people who hate other races. What Springer failed to mention is that it is usually only the obnoxious or outrageous guest who gets air time and that he really doesn't offer an open forum for the average, "boring," thoughtful, or reticent applicant. More important, no one has a First Amendment right to appear on a show. The First Amendment guarantees only one's right to speak, not to be heard!

Springer is certainly not alone in this strange combination of exploitation and self-righteousness on the part of those involved in the day-to-day production of their shows. In November 1995, Abt had the chance to "debate" Geraldo Rivera on the CBS program *This Morning*. When it was suggested, on air, that he had demonstrated on CNBC's *Rivera Live* that he could do entertaining *and* nontrashy shows, he responded that his CNBC show was "overrated" while his daytime NBC talk show was misunderstood by critics. In other words, he forcefully defended his daytime show. And yet, only a few months later he was reportedly talking about the need for "self-regulation." *USA Today*'s Jeannie Williams wrote in January 1996 that Geraldo had created a "Bill of Rights and Responsibilities" for talk-show hosts that "he hoped Phil, Montel and Maury would adhere to" (2D). He was quoted as saying that he would use this statement to retool his daytime show beginning in the fall of 1996. Curiously, he reiterated his contempt for "zealots seeking attention" who have criticized his daytime show in the past, while at least indirectly, doing so himself. It should not be too surprising that Geraldo's first show of the 1996 season was really just more of the old Geraldo. Mouthing platitudes about "compassion" and "healing," he devoted the program to interviewing convicted felon Joey Buttafuoco and his victim-wife, Mary Jo.

Thus, television's talk shows continue to play dangerous games with mainstream America. In the name of ratings and revenues, they break rules, divert our attention to the most extreme forms of private and public misbehavior, and generally redefine our conceptions of what constitutes acceptable and appropriate reactions to such displays. In the process they erase distinctions between fame and infamy, hero and celebrity, therapy and exploitation, intimate and stranger, sickness and irresponsibility, and perhaps most troubling, any distinction between fact and fiction.

Inappropriate, even pathological, talk and behavior are certainly not modern creations, but technology—notably television—has seen to it that they have entered our homes and become daily houseguests. In the process, we have become all too comfortable with them as we use them for our entertainment. The question of how society should use the power of technology is avoided by the simplistic reliance on popularity and ratings. We may be paying too high a cultural price for television's ability to give us the entertainment we want. That these shows tend to become travesties of their former shocking selves is perhaps evidence that we have indeed become increasingly desensitized to their pathologies. It doesn't seem too much of a stretch of the imagination to assume that they have in some measure contributed to what social commentator Jeffrey Goldfarb has called "The Cynical Society." Surely, they seem to embody some of our society's most worrisome trends, from a general decline in civility to the currently debated decline in literacy.[5]

Historically, societies have always had to put in place mechanisms to control the "deviant" behavior of those who violate their standards and, beyond that, to limit the influence of such people on others. One such social protection has been the limitation of public exposure to violations of convention. Another has been the labeling of such behavior as "beyond the pale," with corresponding public stigma and private feelings of shame. In other words, culture contains social control. Mass culture, however, dependent as it is on technology and commercial interests, has undermined these social controls. Since its inception, television has had the ability to eliminate the physical boundaries of time and place, and talk television has gone much further, rapidly eroding the boundaries that we have established to control behavior and to make sense out of life.

Indeed, the very reasons that brought about the age of talk shows—most notably the need for cheap programming—still exist. Originally talk shows were relied on because, under the "finsyn" rules of the Federal Communications Commission (FCC) put in place in the 1970s, networks were prohibited from producing and airing shows during some hours for their affiliates. Thus, the affiliates were forced to turn to the expanding syndication market to fill the hours previously occupied by their networks. Moreover, station affiliates could now make more money by purchasing and airing syndicated programs, which provided more local advertising minutes for sale than network shows did. At the same time, the networks, faced with dwindling profits, reduced the amount of compensation they offered affiliates for airing network programs. Many of the new programs offered by syndicators were talk shows simply because they were relatively inexpensive to produce. A sixty-minute talk show costs around $50,000 an episode compared to the $1 million price tag for a highly successful sitcom or better-than-average drama (Heaton and Wilson 35).

Today, with new changes in the FCC, networks are once again able to program and distribute shows, a move that helps to explain, for example, Disney's interest in purchasing Capital Cities/ABC now that Hollywood would not be tapped by stations to provide material directly and networks can once again have enormous power over production and distribution. By the same token, however, the high cost of these corporate takeovers in the communications industry in 1996 will spur incentive to continue producing inexpensive shows. As Mitchell Shapiro of the University of Miami emphasizes in his Broadcasting 101 course, TV is a commercial medium, and the programs are not really the product (Jicha C8). The viewers are the real product, and this particular product is sold to advertisers. Ratings thus become the indication of how many viewers a station has to "sell." Put another way, Oprah's Nielsen rating in 1994 was 8.9, with each point representing about one million viewers (Greenberg et al. 2). Couple the staggering size of this audience with the relative cheapness to the station that purchases the program from the syndicator, and the commercial appeal of talk shows becomes obvious. Any other reason offered for their existence on the part of their producers (e.g., information, entertainment, social helpfulness) is simply a smoke screen. Financial considerations drive programming.

This book examines talk television as a microcosm of American popular culture and the commercial interests that manufacture and sustain it. The general lack of restraint and responsibility highlighted on these shows seems matched by that of its producers and syndicators. At a time when government regulation and oversight of the industry is at an all-time low, by necessity, emphasis must be on developing voluntary self-restraint. As the recent Telecommunications Act further loosens restrictions on media mergers and acquisitions, informed media consumers need to contribute their own sustained pressure on producers and government to keep their eyes on the public's interest rather than merely the bottom line. We hope to act here as "media ecologists," informing the reader's judgment and developing what Brian Stonehill has called "media literacy." "Censorship will cease to be a danger," Stonehill wrote in a 1995 opinion piece for *The Philadelphia Inquirer*, "and the ratings-driven culture might even start to improve—fancy that!—when the audience gets more screen smart and can tell the difference between what's worth noting and what's worth nothing. A wave of such objective and nonideological 'media literacy'—one that enabled people to watch out for what they watch—just might make the culture wars themselves start to fade" (A11). Our hope is that this book will be one of many that help people become just that—more "screen smart."

In the first half of this book, our intent is to show how the "game" of talk television works. The second half looks at the behind-the-scenes games and their implications, as well as what we as a culture might do to protect ourselves from their deceptions and misinformation. We deal with the complex commercial and political interests motivating their production, particularly at a time when media mergers are at an all time high and political action has done little to mitigate the dangers of such a powerful source of cultural messages. In the appendix is a detailed description of the corporate players and the revenues they are generating.

Finally, it doesn't matter whether the reader is interested in talk shows per se, nor for that matter, is it important that our culture will eventually grow tired of them, and they will cease to draw an audience. The point is that the transformation of TV talk shows over time is the quintessential illustration of the ways in which material culture (technology, the media) affects our cultural narratives and symbols and, through them, changes the *social construction of reality*. This influence is a perfect example of what McLuhan meant by "the medium *is* the message."

Notes

1. For a good "first-hand account" of the quiz-show scandal by the district attorney involved, see Joseph Stone and Tim Yohn's *Prime Time and Misdemeanors: Investigating the 1950's TV Show Scandals: A DA's Account*. The book is the basis of Robert Redford's film *Quiz Show*.

2. The research was part of an ongoing study of popular culture and television programming. Content analysis was conducted using three nationally syndicated, "mainstream" talk shows aired in the Philadelphia area on the ABC affiliate station over a six-month period. For a period of four weeks during the latter part of November and the early part of December 1991, each episode of these talk shows was viewed and coded as to subject, format, commercial breaks, participants, interaction patterns, and dialogue. A total of sixty shows—twenty episodes each of *Donahue, Sally Jessy Raphael,* and *The Oprah Winfrey Show*—were transcribed, coded and analyzed from video tapes. From December 1991 to June 1992, programs were occasionally viewed to see if substantive changes in format had occurred. With the exception of a few interviews with Presidential candidates, these shows continued to focus on individuals' violations of private and public behavioral norms. No attempt was made to contrast the three talk shows as the differences, at the time, were considered largely to be stylistic rather than substantive. Even today, as indicated by the various shows that are used as illustrations throughout this book, the programs are basically equivalent; hence a "random" sampling of shows seems unnecessary to make the point. In effect, with a few notable exceptions, if you've seen one, you've seen them all.

3. Criticism in the popular print media, only some of which we specifically mention in the book, includes the following: Vicki Abt, "Conservatives Have Abetted the TV Trash," *The Philadelphia Inquirer*, 19 November 1995: E7; "Phil, Sally, Oprah Drag Society Down," *The New York Daily News*, 4 September 1994: C19; Kurt Anderson, "Pop Goes the Culture," *Time*, 16 June 1986: 68-74; Tad Friend, "White Trash Nation," *New York* cover story, 22 August 1994; Gina Bellafante, "Playing Get the Guest," *Time*, 27 March 1995: 77; William Grimes, "The Deconstruction of Jenny, Maury and Montel," *The New York Times*, 10 December 1995: E7; Maureen Dowd, "Talk Is Cheap," *The New York Times*, 26 October 1995: A25; Ellen Gray, "Hey, It's OK! I Saw It on TV: Are These People Talking Us into Deviant Behavior?" *The Philadelphia Daily News*, 14 July 1994: 46, 48; Janice Kaplan, "Are Talk Shows Out of Control?" *TV Guide,* 1 April 1995: 10-15; Elizabeth

Kolbert, "Wages of Deceit: Untrue Confessions," *The New York Times*, 11 June 1995, Arts and Leisure 129; Bob Lacayo, "Violent Reaction: Bob Dole's Broadside against Sex and Violence in Popular Culture Sets Off a Furious Debate on Responsiblity," *Time*, 12 June 1995: 30-35; David Ruben, "New Trouble on TV," *Parenting*, October 1995: 21; Stephen Seplow, "Now, They're Talking about Talk Shows," *The Philadelphia Inquirer*, 12 March 1995: A4; Stephen Seplow, "Seduced and Abandoned: If You Tell All on TV, Do You Find Catharsis? Or More Headaches?" *The Philadelphia Inquirer Magazine*, 24 September 1995: 12-14+; Stephen Seplow, "Titans of Talk Are Pressured to Get Kinks Out of Daytime TV," *The Philadelphia Inquirer*, 5 November 1995: A1, A19; Marilyn Stasio, "When Talk Shows Become Horror Shows," *Cosmopolitan*, October 1995: 250-53; Mary Talbot, "Talk Shows on the Brain," *The New York Daily News*, 30 July 1995: 3-5; Jane Whitney, "When Talk Gets Too Cheap," *U.S. News and World Report*, 12 June 1995: 57-58; and Cathy Young, "Talk Shows Aren't the Problem: They Are Reflecting Our Culture," *The Philadelphia Inquirer*, 19 November 1995: E7.

4. Among the many who have written recently about this general "dumbing" of America are Robert Bly, *The Sibling Society* (Lexington: Addison-Wesley 1996); Katharine Washburn and John Thornton, eds, *Dumbing Down: Essays on the Strip Mining of American Culture* (New York: Norton, 1996); Tom Shachtman, *The Inarticulate Society: Eloquence and Culture in America* (New York: Free Press, 1995); William A. Henry, 3rd, *In Defense of Elitism* (New York: Doubleday, 1995); and Gary Taylor, *Cultural Selection* (New York: Basic Books, 1996).

5. Cultural commentators who have recently written on the general decline in civility and citizenship standards include journalist Georgie Ann Geyer in *Americans No More: The End of Citizenship* (New York: Grove/Atlantic, 1996), and former Supreme Court nominee Robert Bork in *Slouching towards Gomorrah: Modern Liberalism and American Decline* (New York: HarperCollins, 1996).

1

Contaminating Culture

Unless we recognize that television in the main is being used to distract, delude, amuse and insulate us, then television and those who finance it, look at it, and those who work at it, may see a totally different picture of the world too late.
> —Edward R. Murrow, Radio and Television
> News Directors Convention, Chicago (1958)

When television is bad, nothing is worse. . . . Keep your eyes glued to that set until the station signs off. I can assure you that you will observe a vast wasteland.
> —Newton Minow, former chair of the FCC (1961)

With television . . . the artificial-information field is brought inside our darkened rooms, inside our stilled minds, and shot by cathode guns through our moving eyes into our brains and recorded. We have no participatory role in gathering data. . . . [W]e become a hermit in the cave who knows only what the TV offers.
> —Jerry Mander, *Four Arguments*
> *for the Elimination of Television* (1978)

Rather than rush to judgment of social behavior, as was once all too common, we rush from judgment, disposed to justify or overlook the most appalling lapses.
> —James Morris, "The Rise and Fall of Civility"
> *Wilson Quarterly* Fall 1996

Scenario: Karen decides that she can no longer hide her dark secret from Bob, her husband of six years. While experiencing the illicit ecstacy of the most satisfying and personally fulfilling sex she's ever known, she's also harbored painful feelings and another vague, atrophied emotion. She thinks it used to be called "shame."

Why should she have to live with this feeling? After all, wasn't it her life anyway? Wasn't her first obligation to herself? How could she love someone else if she didn't love herself first? Hadn't she read all the "self-help" books in the drugstore? After all, wasn't this the '90s? After all . . .

She decides that it's time to "come out of the closet." She knows the revelation will be devastating to Bob, but he has to hear it nevertheless. Whether he'd admit it to himself or not, her confession would set them both free. Confession was good for the soul, wasn't it?

The problem, of course, is how to tell him. Should she blurt it out over dessert one evening? Take him away to the country and break it on a peaceful walk in the woods? After two weeks of agonized pondering, the answer comes to her. It is right there under her nose all the time, right there in the convenience store where she works as a cashier, right there on television. Why hadn't she thought of it before? It is perfect, just what she needs, what they need—a professional ear to listen and advise and a supportive group to help heal the wounds of injurious words. She dials the 800 number, and it's all set. Now how to get him there. Deception, which had gotten her this far, would be a big help.

"Bob, I've been seeing someone," she tells him defiantly after they're comfortably seated at the professional's place of business.

He remains remarkably calm, as the group murmurs its disapproval of her revelation. "I knew it," he says after a long pause. "I had a feeling. Who is he?"

Now for the really hard part, for he knew her lover well . . . very well. She hesitates, and the professional urges her on, telling her what she already knows—that confession is good for the soul, that it will make them all feel better. Honest!

"It's not a he,*" Karen says, almost whispering.*

"She?" he asks, locking eyes with hers, his former composure giving way to tremulous emotion.

"Yes, she," *Karen says, calmer now as the balm of confession begins its work. Her friend the professional was right about the effect of such confession. She goes on, more daring now: "And not just any she. It's your sister, Ellen. We're in love. I'm sorry."*

The group sputters to life, but the professional calms them. There would be time later for their responses. For now he wants to

*know how Bob feels. "How do you feeeel about what you've just
heard your wife say, Bob," he coos. Bob balks, and the professional lets him know, ever gently, that non-response is counterpro-
ductive, not acceptable. Tentatively, he speaks—shock, outrage,
betrayal, sin, perversion, hellfire, damnation. . . . Hold that
thought, the professional asserts. More after these messages. The
group waits patiently for three minutes to pass. They are, after all,
a supportive group . . . a large supportive group . . . a large supportive group of about two hundred! And beyond them, wired into
the global village, a larger group still—about ten million![1]*

It is, of course, impossible to satirize what is already parody
and travesty, and however bizarre this fictional scenario might
seem, anyone who watches television talk shows knows that it is
not far from the actual game-like format of these enormously
popular programs. In fact, it's mild compared to some of the real
talk shows that we'll be describing throughout this book. Jerry
Springer's contribution to the Independence Day festivities in
1995 was to rerun a program on "Club Kids," ten self-mutilating
transvestites prancing around on stage while the rowdy audience
was on its feet cheering them on. And then, of course, there's the
sensationalized murder case related to the shocking revelation that
took place during the taping of *The Jenny Jones Show*. It was to be
a program about people with secret crushes on others. Hoping to
meet a young lady with an interest in him, Michigan waiter
Jonathan Schmitz, 24, was shocked to learn that his secret admirer
was actually a young male acquaintance, a gay bartender named
Scott Amedure. Schmitz was apparently so disturbed by the
encounter that, three days after the show's taping on March 6,
1995, he visited Amedure's trailer home and shot him to death,
later telling the police that the humiliation that he experienced on
national TV had "eaten away" at him. This murder was only one
of the estimated 30,000 committed in the United States each year,
but it garnered worldwide headlines.[2]

Interestingly, this case is exceptional not only because it
involves an outrageous felonious act, but also because it is not typical of the reaction that the majority of talk-show "guests" have to
their own embarrassing experiences on the air. On the contrary,
most volunteer to participate despite possible embarrassment for a

variety of reasons that make the risks seem worthwhile. In April 1995, for instance, Abt appeared on *The Marilyn Kagan Show* (KCAL Los Angeles) in a program titled "Talk Show Madness," which was supposed to deal with the social fallout of these shows and their misuse of the therapeutic model.[3] In fact, it featured a variety of former talk-show guests, some of whom were dissatisfied with their experiences and yet still willing to tell their stories on television once again, and some who were quite satisfied with their experiences. There is no way to know whether these guests were a representative sample of the total population of talk-show participants, and so the fact that they were evenly split may only represent the producers' desires to have a "balanced show." Included were the following:

- A mother who had publicly criticized her daughter's sexual promiscuity and now wished she hadn't. Kagan told the mother and daughter to "talk to each other" and then to hug and forgive each other—right there in front of the other guests, the studio audience, and the thousands of people tuned in at home. They seemed confused throughout the taping.

- A woman who had used a national talk show to reveal to her boyfriend the affairs that she had had while they were together. Kagan wanted the bewildered man to forgive and forget on the spot. When asked how he felt after his girlfriend had made the shocking revelation, he just mumbled a lot, indicating that he didn't know what to think.

- A woman who had talked about her sexual exploits on a talk show. She now complained that her reputation in her home town was ruined and that she had also lost her boyfriend as a result of her brush with fame.

- A woman without legs who found her experience talking about her sexuality on a talk show exciting. She told the audience that she now had plenty of dates and was starting a group devoted to "sex and deformity."

- A woman who went from one talk show to another "advertising" herself to wealthy men. She asserted that there was nothing wrong in thinking that you were beautiful and classy (she seemed to be neither) and that she had met many men who were willing to support her.

• A former KKK member who, having seen the error of his ways, went from talk show to talk show to preach his message of love. Although this message seemed quite muddled and he seemed more involved with his own fame than with his promotion of love, the studio audience applauded him enthusiastically.

The point here is that people appear on talk shows for many different reasons, including their desire to "explain" themselves, to use the shows to get even with other guests they have persuaded to appear with them, to reunite with people who might not want to be reunited with them, and perhaps most commonly, to satisfy their need/desire for attention, which no medium can provide better than television. Whether they are victims or victimizers is immaterial. Even if most guests are satisfied after appearing on these shows, it is the viewing audience—the millions of people who watch and listen—who are being deceived and manipulated by their words and behavior. Ultimately, it is American culture itself that is being victimized by these breaches of common boundaries between public and private, fame and infamy, therapy and confession. Bernice Kanner, a frequent contributor to *The New York Times*, in writing about a study she had done on Americans' attitudes toward lying, has correctly observed that it seems people are more accepting now than ever of exaggeration, falsification, misstatements, misrepresentations, glossovers, quibbles, concoctions, equivocations, shuffles, prevarications (43-44). Television talk, which surely helps to feed this tolerance for deception, is not simply silly, tasteless, grammatically incorrect, or vulgar. It is, we believe, recklessly toxic to our attitudes and culture.

"Americans Despair of Popular Culture," reads the headline of an article by Elizabeth Kolbert in the Sunday, August 20, 1995, issue of *The New York Times*. The article notes that Americans worry about sex and violence on television and that "they believe there is a direct connection between the fictional world young people are exposed to and the way they behave in real life." "Fictions," or the stories we tell, certainly help create the social "blueprints" of our behavior in real life. What is interesting, however, is that while most Americans at least acknowledge the dangers of violent and sexual images on television and in the movies, they do not appear to be as concerned with the words and images that make up the deceptive world of "reality-based" talk television. The blurring of the worlds of fiction and reality is a recurring theme throughout this book. Surely long-term exposure to this genre has consequences for the way we judge ideas, behaviors, and "values" and the way we respond to "deviance" in terms of defining it, emulating it, or mitigating it. Toxic talk may not seem as obvious in its effects as brutal violence and impersonal sex on the screen, but we believe it is at least as devastating to society at large. Consider what we are watching when we tune in to talk TV:

- Lies, misinformation, and incomplete information about "guests" as instigated or "enabled" by the celebrity-host

- Extreme close-ups of highly personal moments, including family "reunions," surprise encounters, and "outings"

- Wild audience cheering and laughing at inane or "deviant" behavior and responses to questions

- Interruptions of emotionally devastating stories for commercial breaks

- Intimate tales of personal turmoil out of the context of the confessants' ordinary lives

- Audience and guest obsession with extreme, socially uncontrolled behavior

- Guests treated as categories or types in a gallery of social grotesques

- Obliviousness to major social and political issues in favor of "confession"

- Sound-bite pop psychology to address serious pathologies

- Contempt for intellectuals and intellectual debate

- Poor grammar, limited vocabulary, and cliché-ridden language

- Fact undifferentiated from unsupported opinion

- Ignorance of the relationships among manners, morals, and behavior

- The replacement of a sense of history with interest only in personal biography and/or autobiography

- "Victims" obsessed with themselves and seemingly unaware of norms of conduct or etiquette whose violations may contribute to their "victimization"

- Near-monopolistic empires built on our morbid fascination with the dysfunctional and defended on the grounds of "equality" and "free speech"

The deceptions and contradictions are perhaps best exemplified in a September 1995 promo for the 1995-96 season of *The Montel Williams Show*. With words and faces flashing on the screen, the announcer proclaims, "RACIST, SEXIST, ACTIVIST . . . Montel brings us together. SURVIVOR, DECEIVER, BELIEVER . . . It starts with talk; it ends with answers. Montel brings us together." One can only assume from this "message" that there are really no significant differences among us that can't be smoothed over by entertaining talk. (Montel must have been on to something as his show won the daytime Emmy for "best talk show of 1995.") In the 1995-1996 season, Montel continued this "therapeutic vein" with a May 1996 program featuring men bragging about having had sex with underaged girls (the girls *and* their mothers were on stage). Messages were then broadcast during the commercial breaks asking, "Are you a teen girl whose parents have kicked you out of the house? If so, call Montel." We can only conclude from this solicitation that the viewing public can expect more shows about the entertaining topic of exploited underage girls.

Surely long-term exposure to these "entertainments" threatens to alter our experience of the reality of social life and ultimately to remake society in its own muddled image. Talk television represents one of the fastest-growing segments of the mass-entertainment market, reaching always lower for emotional jolts, blithely consumed daily by millions. Its subject matter is akin to what Hannah Arendt called "the banality of evil." What was originally shocking has become commonplace, and to achieve the same novel effect—the hook that gets people to watch what they were not intended to see or shouldn't see, at least publicly—legitimate producers have become, in effect, "the new pornographers."[4] In this cultural context "pornography" implies pandering and commercialism relating to the production and broadcast of material devoid of authentic emotional contexts and calculatedly designed to titillate. Sexual messages are not essential characteristics in this meaning, but rather the cynical distortion of culture for sale.

Of course, the FCC and the courts have not used this standard but have drawn legal distinctions among the terms *obscenity*, *indecency*, and *pornography*. They define indecent programming as material that contains "patently offensive" language as measured by contemporary community standards or material that depicts sexual or excretory activities or organs. By this definition, indecency is regarded as something milder than obscenity or pornography, which feature graphic pictures or descriptions of sex. Such material has been prohibited on broadcast television since the medium's inception, the FCC's rationale being that broadcast signals come into the home "uninvited." Thus, consideration for the nature of its entire audience is in order. Cable TV and the print media are not subject to the same restrictions. This helps to explain the decision by federal judges in Philadelphia to strike down the "decency" section of the 1996 Telecommunications Act with regard to the Internet on the basis that the Internet is "mass speech" and cannot be so regulated. In this way it is more like print and less like television. We discuss this issue again in chapter 7.[5] Contrast this decision with the fact that, as recently as June 1995, a federal appeals court in Washington *upheld* regulations that prohibit radio and television stations from carrying sexually explicit "indecent" programs between the hours of 6 A.M. and 10 P.M. This narrow 7-4 decision essentially preserved restrictions that Congress imposed in 1933, maintaining that government had a "compelling interest" to shield children from indecent programs and material beamed over the airwaves.

But what about the toxic talk shows, which regularly feature indecent and offensive language and obscenely graphic descriptions of incest, rape, and the like? Of course, the appellate court apparently did not take such programming into consideration in its decision because, by definition, appellate courts can deal only with the specific cases and facts before them. Nevertheless, this programming is available during the very hours of the day that the court cited as restricted time. Indeed, with small variations in the major markets, it is available throughout the day. Apparently, the FCC is not paying close attention, and, as a result, the obscenity grows more and more blatant.

There is a legal difference between obscenity and pornography as the Supreme Court defined those terms for First Amendment purposes. However, sociologically and semantically—in other words, culturally—the differences between them are not so great. Obscene material in legal terms is lewd, indecent, and offensive to modesty. As Erving Goffman defined it in *Frame Analysis,* pornography concerns the scripting of sexuality that is "improperly explicit" for the frame in question. As such, this material "makes a public exhibition of private phenomena. . . . When the intimacies of life are exposed to public view, their value may be depreciated, or they may be exposed to public view in order to depreciate them and to depreciate man" (56). Although not as obvious as in the case of X-rated movies or some rap music, television talk shows represent a new pornography as they turn private affairs into public displays, make spectacles of people in order to sell commercial products, showcase deviance for our amusement, and play a deceptive game under the guise of truth, not to mention the general exclusion of entirely normal, functional behavior. Pornography generally involves turning people into objects and making public what is private. Talk shows do precisely that and present a cynical, exhaustive cataloging of self-destructive behavior without benefit of comprehension or context.

Examples abound. Virtually every program description with which we begin the chapters of this book reveals inappropriate, indecent, even pornographic talk and behaviors. Sometimes, the indecency takes subtler, even cute, forms, and is therefore all the more disturbing than the frontal assaults of the "down and dirty" hosts. For example, CBS's *The Gordon Elliott Show* in August 1995 ran a segment titled "Father's Funky Feet." With her parents sitting beside her, looking slightly uncomfortable but also proud of her open admission, a precocious young girl talks about how she has to massage her dad's feet. Her only wish, she adds, is that he would wash them first because his feet are "stinky." The host and the audience laugh appreciatively at this statement, but no one stops to mention that the behavior described is, at best, inappropriate; at worst, it constitutes a form of child abuse.

Programs like this showcase the hideously personal, the trivial, the ludicrous, and the socially insignificant ideas that are the hallmarks of what is sometimes referred to as *low class* behavior—not to mention cognitive and linguistic errors that so tellingly distinguish certain people. The winner-take-all aspect of our information age is maintained by these newly important criteria for class divisions. Although often a result of economic deprivation and educational disadvantage, both of which contribute to poor work prospects, *low class* in this sense refers to norms, values, language, and behaviors and not necessarily to economics as such. By their behavior, rich people can also be considered low class while most poor people need not be. Lifestyle and not money is the determining variable. By watching, participating in, and enjoying these talk-show spectacles, people effectively become low class while doing nothing to understand the social forces that contribute to this dysfunctional culture or to the dysfunctional families that talk shows love to exhibit.

New York Times critic Walter Goodman writes that "by any reasonable standard, the programs, combinations of party games and confrontation therapy, are repulsive. . . . [They] are freak shows, with exhibitions of dysfunction in many forms, often with a sexual twist, run by shameless hucksters who are never more disgusting than when they are pretending to sympathize with the poor creatures they are displaying to a studio audience that is encouraged to whoop encouragement and howl displeasure" (C15). He says later in the piece that this kind of show features "people who seem to come from some contemporary version of Dickens' London. . . . What they lack in grammar they make up in volume. . . . It's a quick jolt of fame before going back to being single mothers or neighborhood drifters" (C21). But he also indicates that what upsets middle-class political critics like William Bennett, the former secretary of education, and others is that when we watch these shows we are forced to confront the class divisions in our society, to confront the "issue of class." Does Goodman think this class awareness rescues the shows? There must be a better way to highlight the class divisions within America without making people into participants in a daily assault on all classes. In fact they just might be making the middle class less so, or more smug rather than sympathetic with the unfortunates paraded before us. It may turn out that after some ten years of watching this kind of programming, the so-called class divisions become more theoretical than actual as we all engage more frequently in behaviors that undermine public civility and logical and scientific standards for rhetoric and debate.

On the other hand, Barbara Ehrenreich, feminist, social theorist, and author of *Fear of Falling*, in an analysis of middle-class culture, has a different interpretation of the talk shows' implications for America's class divisions. She defends the programs, in effect, by likening them to "morality plays" in which the lower classes who appear on these shows are "shown up" at the end and rejected by the studio audiences for their violations of middle-class norms and boundaries. Even if this is indeed the case—and it is typically not, since often those in the audience agree with the conclusions of those on stage in the latter's defense of, or pride in, their "lower class" behaviors and attitudes—the broadcasting of half-truths based on ignorance or malice cannot be undone by some minutes of incomplete attack by audience or host. The words have been said, and many listening in at home may have only caught those that are most titillating.

Of course, those profiting from these displays have good commercial reasons to plumb these class issues. *Entertainment Weekly* estimated that the annual revenues of talk shows top a half billion dollars. NBC News reporter Betty Rollins, in an October 27, 1995 segment on *Empower America*'s attack on talk shows, estimated that revenues were closer to a billion dollars. America may no longer manufacture and export toasters and television sets, but it certainly does manufacture and export entertainment, American "culture." As *Newsweek*'s August 14, 1995, special report on the Disney Company's acquisition of Capital Cities/ABC put the matter, "Entertainment is not just one of America's largest exports, it's also our culture gone global" (21). And what is it that we are selling the world? In the case of talk TV, we are selling entertainment that derives from self-serving confession, cruel deception, public loss of social control, bad manners and diction, distortions and misrepresentations of reality, exhibitionism, the flagrant high-lighting of deviance, and even murder. We are also telling them that this is what we are as Americans and what they should aspire to in their admiration of our "culture."

Regrettably, TV's talk shows display many of the contradictions or, less charitably, hypocrisies of a toxic culture gone amok, a culture out of touch with reality, either by denying that such a thing as external reality exists or ignoring it. In fact, they may be less revealing of dysfunctional individuals than they are of a society that, at the very least, has grown cynical and tasteless, at worst of one that seems to have altogether forgotten what is real and what illusory. Other distinctions are blurred as well to suit commercial and entertainment ends as the hosts and producers carry out their roles, alternating disingenuously between view-points:

- Between sympathy for and exploitation of their guest-victims

- Between cynicism toward and naivete about the "deviant" behavior the guests exhibit

- Between mouthing simplistic platitudes about hope and hope-lessness about the "system"

- Between showcasing class-based differences and making insincere assertions about freedom, democracy, equality, cultural relativity, and a classless society

- Between sexual titillation of audience and guest and puritani-cal censure of those who admit to enjoying the dysfunctional sexuality being featured (e.g., incest, mate swapping, trans-sexuality)

- Between expressing concern for children and exploiting these very children by having them and their parents act out or witness their familial dysfunctions (e.g., parental arguments, parents prying into the secrets of their children's lives)

- Between claiming to abhor violence and encouraging violent displays by and among guests and an obsessive interest in such behavior

- Between an expressed contempt for realistic limits on human behavior and employing a format that severely limits comprehension and interaction by squeezing dialogue between commercial breaks, confining discussion to one aspect of a person's life to the exclusion of all other factors, and the like

- Between asserting the need for behavioral boundaries and eradicating many social boundaries in pursuit of ratings through shock appeal

- Between the physical make-overs and other simplistic, narcissistic self-improvements offered as remedies for dysfunctionality and the hosts' own knowledge that, if anything, only cultural "make-overs" through education will help these people

The topics, format, and conversation considered reasonable, entertaining, and practical on talk television make the quiz-show scandal of the 1950s look innocent by comparison: Skinheads, racists, misogynists, youngsters who hate school and society, parents who hate their children, self-mutilators, cheating lovers, sadomasochistic lovers, incest perpetrators and "survivors," transsexuals and bisexuals, nymphomaniacs, dysfunctional families all too willing to air their dirty laundry in public, strippers, people with gross eating disorders, astrologists, space travelers, cult members, murderers. . . . The contempt and expoitation of producers for participants and audience is most evident in the motley mix of serious with the simply stupid, with the few minutes of air time devoted to each "guest" regardless of the complexity or superficiality of their story. With their familiar settings, predictable formats, and star hosts who bring in loyal viewers, these shows trivialize dysfunctionality and "deviance" to the point where evil indeed becomes ordinary or banal and where the shocking or unexpected becomes something like manageable "soap opera." Poseurs play for voyeurs, and most go home (or, more often, stay home) satisfied— or so they may think.

Although these devices for amusing us are disturbing in themselves, our concerns are not restricted here to topics and formats, however outlandish, but the varieties of toxic talk as such, which are as disconcerting. In an episode of *The Sally Jessy Raphael Show* entitled "Mom Doesn't Wear Enough Clothes," a 19-year-old girl named Shannon and her mother, Nina, 48, talk to Sally and the audience. Under them, a chyron or subtitle flashes: "Shannon Says Her Mother Dresses Like a Slut." Nina, who has been twice married to men of 21 and 26, says laughingly that, in order to sabotage her relationship with men much younger than she, her daughter "picks her nose and wipes it on their clothes. Another time [ha ha] she even flushed my diaphram down the toilet [ha ha]." On another channel the same day, *The Gordon Elliott Show* featured the topic "My Best Friend Won't Stop Hitting on Me." One female says of another young woman who was "hitting on her" in the health club where they both work, "You should see her boobs." The toxic talk in these illustrations includes only a couple of the varieties one is likely to hear on such shows. These varieties include:

- Disgusting talk

- Misinformation

- Hate talk (racism, anti-Semitism, sexism)

- Poor English ("Youse don't know nothing"; "I seen it"; "He done that"; "Why you be doin' this?")[6]

- Mean talk ("I hate you. You're a whore.")

- Personal talk

- Telling of shocking secrets

- Shouting matches, even physical confrontations

- Profanity, with inserted "bleeps" through which we can read lips

As has been pointed out, many of us, including politicians, educators, and journalists, express concern about this electronic confessional/sideshow/freak show/Roman circus, but fail to address the evolution of the genre, the ways in which it operates, its financial infrastructure, its dependency on the medium of television, and its effects on American civilization. In a July 18, 1995, *New York Times* piece, Russell Baker terms a curse "technology's tendency to separate people from the consequences of their worst behavior" (A13). In another *New York Times* Op-Ed on October 26, 1995, Maureen Dowd also reports on William Bennett's attack on TV talk shows after the conservatives' success in getting Time Warner to sell its gangsta rap label. However belated Bennett's discovery of "America's true heart of darkness: daytime TV talk shows," Dowd also decries the "values" of a genre that celebrates "publicity over achievement, revelation over restraint, honesty over decency, victimhood over personal responsibility, confrontation over civility [and] psychology over morality" (A25). (The irony of the conservative attack on commercial popular culture is not lost on us, however much we agree with the criticism.) Mark Slouka, in his recently published *War of the Worlds: Cyberspace and the High-Tech Assault on Reality* goes further and suggests that without the checks and balances of the real world, our worst tendencies can be acted upon. Television does both as it enables us to escape into its own "virtual reality," creating a substitute or ersatz society. We watch television indoors, like people watching shadows on Plato's cave walls, but it is surely dangerous to mistake our own "electronic caves" for the outside world that we must finally return to and deal with.

Before television, people could not easily satisfy a desire for gossip or their voyeurism without risking their own reputations or physical safety by having to travel to circuses, side shows, red-light districts, flophouses, and other unsafe and/or illegal places and come into contact with dangerous people. This inconvenience placed natural limits on appetite. Of course, there were also safer ways to obtain pornographic material—books and films—but they came with their own built-in constraints. For one, you needed to know how to read, or you had to go to a movie theater to consume the other. Moreover, the printed page and the darkened theater became frame mechanisms in themselves, reminding you continually that what you were looking at was not real life. But television has all but removed these apparent dangers, social curbs to deviant appetite, and artistic constraints.

As McLuhan asserted in the early 1960s, the medium *is* the message, and talk shows with their game-like format and dramatized conflicts fit the television medium's possibilities while refusing to deal with television's own inability to represent complex ideas. These programs appear to be innocent and safe enough, their messages coming as they do out of the innocuous little boxes we keep in our family rooms and bedrooms. Other distortions of reality come out of that little box, too. Disney started out by making adorable little characters for movie theaters (not to mention staggering sums of money) out of rodents, but then again, Disney dealt with animated fictions, not with real people. (With the new media conglomerate that Disney is now becoming, however, that may change, too.) The talk shows, by contrast, turn troubled people into victim-celebrities and, ultimately, they threaten to remake the culture that tolerates such a transformation in the name of entertainment. While we create culture, it in turn creates us. It informs our thinking, our feelings, and, ultimately, our actions. When culture changes, so do our psychological and social structures because the three are inherently linked.

The people who invented, packaged, promoted, and embraced this brand of lurid entertainment are creating an America that is a far cry from the one envisioned by the nation's Founders. Worried even then about the degradation of culture, about its sinking to the lowest common denominator, they attempted to build in safeguards against the fickleness and potential tyranny of mass opinion. Ultimately, though, the most effective and most enduring safeguard was thought to be "civil instruction" resulting in an enlightened populace. "A nation that thinks it can be ignorant and free," wrote Thomas Jefferson, "thinks what never was and could never be" (Letter to Col. Charles Yancey, January 6, 1816).

Today opinion polls—many of them based purely on uninformed perception—heavily influence the producers of culture and the politicians who are supposed to ensure the public good by, among other things, regulating media if for no other reason than the limited availability of broadcasting facilities and bands. Popular emotion and materialistic windfall profits alone seem to guide the agenda. Entertainment, rather than reasoned discourse, has become our overiding value, as Postman suggests in *Amusing Ourselves to Death*. The definition of a "good" television show, writes Postman later in *Technopoly*, "has become purely and simply a matter of its having high ratings. . . . There is no need for [it] to consult tradition, aesthetic standards, thematic plausibility, refinements of taste, or even comprehensibility. The iron rule of public opinion is all that matters" (136). The economic windfall, of course, comes to those who pander to popular taste for profit. To quote Jefferson again, "[M]erchants have no country. The mere spot they stand on does not constitute any stronger an attachment as that from which they draw their gains" (Letter to Horatio G. Spafford, March 17, 1814).

Historically, it seems, there has always been an uneasy relationship among economic interests, popular sentiment, and the larger public good. Those who defined the freedoms for political speech provided by the First Amendment could not have foreseen the new set of problems posed by the invention of television and its potential for overwhelming assault upon the carefully balanced system they had designed. Although many of television's critics have discussed the dangers inherent in the medium itself, none of them has adequately addressed the relationship of democracy, commercial television, and mass culture. Television's dominance in the marketplace is staggering. Twenty-four hours a day, seven days a week, judgments based purely on ratings are broadcast to the nation's citizens and, as we export our "product," to the world as well. In fact, the interactive TV broadcasts currently being developed and tested will make it possible for viewers to register opinions as they watch and for producers to compile the data almost instantaneously. And the topics on which viewers can "vote" will not be limited to rating programs, but will include political speeches and news events. Politicians will be able to determine within minutes how their audiences feel about their positions so that they may adjust those positions accordingly. What we will have is a kind of spontaneous plebiscite based purely upon emotional appeal and without benefit of time for reflection, discussion, and study. That is surely not what we need—more decisions based purely on image and emotion rather than measured reasoning and knowledge.

The talk we talk and the games we play are the clearest indicators we have of the processes involved in shaping society, and television provides a clear and disturbing picture of America today. Talk shows, then, can be seen as a kind of social index of America's cultural malaise, which involves, among other things, incivility, inauthentic feelings, illiteracy, lack of citizenship skills, family disorganization, increasingly violent youths, and the stubbornly resistant social ills of minorities and the poor. To an extent, the producers of the toxic-talk shows are right when they say defensively that they are merely reflecting what much of the public wants and knows. (Of course, these same producers don't acknowledge the fact that, in the process, they are also controlling the communications industry, making large sums of money and transforming popular taste by taking it down to ever lower levels.) Human beings are plastic and opportunistic, possessing an unknown number of scenarios by which to live their lives. It follows, then, that broadcasting the worst choices, the worst-case scenarios, must contribute to poor choices and fewer "well-lived" lives. These programs showcase the worst among us (and in us) and offer only superficial glances at better alternatives. They reflect poor taste and poor decision-making at the individual level, and they also reflect the hostile, selfish mood of a growing segment of America.

And what does that America look like in the last decade of the millennium? It is an America that many would argue projects a self-indulgent obsession with the quick fix, with games, with entertainment, and most of all, with the dominance of the individual, even if it means ignoring the viability of the larger society.[7] The therapeutic model seems to have largely replaced character as the basis of personality. In the oversimplified terms of this model, there is no such thing as moral evil or "sin," only undesirable behaviors, victimization, and errors in judgment that can be "fixed" with the right treatment.[8]

It is an America in which the erosion of middle-class economic circumstances has led to the apparent abandonment of the values that used to uphold middle-class life—propriety, delayed gratification, self-control, reticence, and hard work, to name a few.[9]

It is an America in which cultural relativists, deconstructionists, and multiculturalists philosophically argue that there is no such thing as absolute truth (except, of course, their criticism), no objective basis for standards of good and bad, merely competing political interests.[10] Translated into political correctness it is countered by a backlash of moral politics that ignores concrete complaints about real systemic inequities. In fact both sides have substituted all-consuming either/or positions, based on "principle" rather than on the real-life consequences of their extreme positions. Notably absent is the compromise and situational pragmatism of an earlier America.

It is an America in which the underclass, specifically through the medium of television, would seem to have finally "triumphed." Social failures, dropouts, sexual deviants, unmarried mothers, skinheads, misogynists, Nazis, and others without reputations to lose and the attendant consequences of such a loss are exploited for shock effect and made media celebrities, if only for a few minutes, and millions of people a day willingly tune in to be entertained and influenced. But it is also an America in which *The New York Times* on October 27, 1995, reported that the economic gap between the haves and the have-nots is wider than in any other industrial nation (Bradsher D2). On June 20, 1996, *The New York Times* reported again on the subject, saying that the gap between richest and poorest among us is at its greatest since World War II (Holmes A1). The "triumph" of the have-nots is clearly illusory.

It is an America, finally, in which "the traditional categories of cultural life become blurred. . . . [T]he 'factual world' is thus replaced by a world constructed for entertainment and profit" (Gergen 121). Into this cultural vacuum come both consumer-oriented television from one direction and from the other, the "radical right," who themselves talk out of both sides of their mouths— preaching sin and damnation in one breath, and laissez-faire economics, deregulation, even dismantling government itself in the next.

While it is true that this book is a description of television talk shows, it is their relationship to our cultural "blueprints" and to social trends including economic and political factors that are of greatest concern. We deal with talk-show deceptions in chapters 2, 3, and 4 and with the "behind the screen" forces in chapters 5 and 6. An underlying cultural problem in our "blueprints" is our culture's contradictory attitude toward "vice," defining certain behaviors as sinful, making some of them illegal, and then using them for titillation and profit. We consider a crucial question: Why now? What forces, other than decades of exposure to television itself, made it possible for the rise of this type of "entertainment" at this particular moment in our history? Clearly economics is a major force. In a *New York Times* article on the proposed acquisition of Turner Broadcasting by Time Warner (August 31, 1995),

James Sterngold asserts that many are concerned with the increasing concentration of power in fewer hands and fear that "a huge conglomerate would seek consistency and high-volume, high-return productions, rather than gambling on riskier fare like quirky, daring or offbeat films and programs" (D4). Clearly the new media titans offer much to be concerned about, and, in chapter 6, we consider the effect of recent changes in the industry. The book concludes by offering suggestions for what we might do—short of getting rid of our First Amendment rights or our TV sets to remedy the situation.

Notes

1. This first scenario is a fictional compilation of many real talk shows. The last scenario at the beginning of chapter 7 is also fictional. The scenarios at the beginning of chapters 2 through 6, however, were taken from actual shows. As pointed out in the endnotes to the introduction, with slight variations in style, almost all talk-show scenarios are variations on the theme of emotional displays regarding private matters in a seemingly "safe," albeit false, "therapeutic" or helpful public forum. It is the "no sense of place" of much of the goings on that fuel the shows. See Joshua Meyrowitz's 1985 book by that title for a general indictment of the electronic media's effects on social relationships in the real world.

2. Some of the magazine and newspaper stories dealing specifically with the murder include Janice Kaplan, "Are Talk Shows Out of Control? *TV Guide*, April 1-7, 1995: 10-15; "Talk Show Murder," *People*, cover story 27 March 1995; Marilyn Stasio, "When Talk Shows Become Horror Shows," *Cosmopolitan*, October 1995: 250-53; Tod Nissen, "Trial in Slaying of Gay Admirer Spotlights Seedy Side to TV Talk Shows," *The Philadelphia Inquirer*, 7 October 1996: A5; Gail Shister, "Talk Shows Must Chance to Survive, Hosts Say After Murder Verdict," *The Philadelphia Inquirer*, 13 November 1996: D8; and Keith Bradsher, "Talk-Show Guest Guilty of Second-Degree Murder," *The New York Times*, 13 November 1996: A14.

3. The show's producers told Abt over the phone that Marilyn Kagan was a psychotherapist and that, aside from her television program, was in private practice. Excerpts from other Kagan shows often

aired on *Talk Soup* on the E Entertainment cable network (supposedly a parody of these shows but really little more than an excuse to advertise the shows that send in clips and to make fun of the victims for our amusement) belies any truth of this claim, as Kagan behaves just like most of the other hosts with nary a trace of worry about professional protocol or concern over the safeguards built into the private practice of therapeutic counseling.

4. For a relevant historical discussion of the apocryphal warnings about tampering with restraints and boundaries, see Roger Shattuck, *Forbidden Knowledge: From Prometheus to Pornography* (New York: St. Martin's, 1996).

5. According to a *New York Times* article titled "Judges Turn Back Law to Regulate Internet Decency: Free Speech Case," 13 June 1996: 1, the three judges involved in the decision had cited the inherent "chaos and cacophony" of mass speech and granted a temporary restraining order prohibiting the Justice Department from enforcing, or even investigating, violations of the Communications Decency Act's ban on indecent and "patently offensive" speech. "The judges said the Internet deserved at least as much, if not more, protection under the First Amendment as printed material received. The Government had argued that cyberspace should be subject to the stricter regulation given television and radio."

6. In this regard, the recent controversy over "Ebonics" or Black English is pointedly limited. On talk shows, varieties of grammatical errors and misuses abound regardless of racial distinctions.

7. Many are worrying about the general decline in "community" and civic involvement. See especially two books with the same title: Robert N. Bellah et al., *The Good Society* (New York: Vintage Books, 1991); and John Kenneth Galbraith, *The Good Society: The Humane Agenda* (Boston: Houghton Mifflin, 1996).

8. For a discussion of this point, see especially chapters 4 and 5.

9. See especially chapter 5.

10. For one of the most understandable discussions of this conflict, see Kenneth Gergen, *The Saturated Self: Dilemmas of Identity in Contemporary Life* (New York: Basic Books, 1991).

2

Television Plays the "Reality Game"

All the world's a stage,
And all the men and women merely players.
—William Shakespeare

What do you think such people would see of themselves and each other except their shadows, which the fire cast on the opposite wall of the cave? . . . Such persons would certainly believe there were no realities except those shadows of hand-made things.
—Plato, *The Republic*, Book VII

Reality is socially defined. . . . To understand the state of the socially constructed universe at any given time, or its change over time, one must understand the social organization that permits the definers to do their defining.
—Peter Berger and Thomas Luckmann,
The Social Construction of Reality (1967)

Frames give meaning to situations by separating the world into actions that "belong together."
—Erving Goffman, *Frame Analysis* (1974)

Popular culture serves as the grids of perception through which we screen so-called "reality."
—Leslie Fiedler, *Tyranny of the Normal* (1996)

Richard Bey: This episode is meant to be a mocking parody of the old Family Feud *game show, where members of two families competed for cash and prizes by guessing the most frequent responses to innocuous questions like "What's the first thing people do when they get up in the morning?" The original show was hosted by actor Richard Dawson, who greeted the ladies on the panels with a kiss. In his version, Richard Bey kisses no one, for obvious reasons. His version is titled "Dysfunctional Family Feud."*

The blue team is composed of three grossly obese siblings and their toothless elderly grandmother, Dottie. In his introduction, Richard Bey says that the name is appropriate for her, though there is no evidence to suggest that he knows her well enough to comment on her intelligence or presence of mind. But then again, evidence has nothing to do with the judgments made about anyone on the panels. The stereotypes do very nicely.

The all-female pink team is even more obese than their blue counterparts. In fact, by the end of the program, their excess weight would pay dividends. Besides the rowdy studio audience, moreover, the pink sisters have brought their own audience, situated on stage beside them. Dad sits in a chair next to mom, and mom is lying in a hospital bed. Tubes issue from her nose, and she has trouble breathing. She, too, is obese. On the other side of the bed, a woman in a nurse's outfit stands, taking mom's pulse from time to time. We're later told that she's really not a nurse, but a member of Bey's production staff—merely one of many "surprises" in the hour.

The settings feed into the obvious stereotypes being manipulated—"feed" in both the literal and figurative senses. On the panel table in front of each set of contestants are buckets of Kentucky Fried Chicken, boxes of Dunkin' Donuts, bags of Cheetos snacks, and cans of Coke. All of the brand names are clearly visible; all of the contestants eat and drink heartily throughout the program. There are live chickens wandering the stage, pecking at chicken feed, and careful editing ensures juxtaposed shots of these live chickens in the electronic barnyard and fat women eating greasy cooked chicken with their hands. Whenever the enormous male from the blue team moves out in front of the table, elephant sounds are played; when the women from the pink team do the same, a cow is heard mooing. Country banjo music punctuates the breaks in the action.

"Who's the craziest person in your family?" Richard Bey asks to get things going. One responds that it's her sister, who physically assaults anyone in the family, including her own husband and children. Another tops that by saying it's her mother, who feels

her boyfriends' butts whenever the girl takes them home. Her brother, who appears to be far below normal intelligence, agrees that it's their mother who's the craziest, but for a different reason: she forces him to take the "retarded bus" to school.

At this point, the program begins to resemble Family Feud *more directly. The panelists are asked to identify the most frequent audience responses to questions like "What's the most dysfunctional TV family in America?" To help him reveal the answers, Bey brings out an assistant, who plays a kind of Vanna White to his Pat Sajak from the game show* Wheel of Fortune. *"Electra" is her name. She is in her twenties, dressed in spike heels, a very low-cut black top and a very short black miniskirt. An ample amount of bare thigh is exposed between the bottom of the skirt and the tops of slinky black stockings. Electra doesn't say anything or even smile at the camera very much. She doesn't have to.*

The pace of the "action" is accelerated now. An audience member is selected "to pie" anyone on the panel. He picks to shove a cream pie in Bey's face. Grandma Dottie shows the inside of her mouth, replete with false and missing teeth. A member of the blue team partially removes her pants to show her cellulite, and a member of the pink team, not to be outdone, reveals her birthmark by pulling down her pants and revealing her entire backside. At that point, a producer standing off to the right, egging on the rowdy studio audience, looks at her in disgust and holds up a prepared sign that says "Why I'm Gay."

The game concludes with a lightning round to determine a winner. There's a spaghetti-eating contest and a tag-team pillow fight. Finally, it all comes down to their combined weight. The blue team totals 918 pounds. Although the fifteen-year-old male weighs 360 pounds, Grandma Dottie comes in at only 145, and she costs them the victory. The girls of the pink team range in weight from 203 to 319, and their combined total is a whopping 1,021 pounds.

Mom beams proudly from her hospital bed as their prize is announced—a weekend at beautiful Mt. Airy Lodge in the Pocono Mountains of Pennsylvania, a romantic haven for frugal honeymooners replete with oversized heart-shaped tubs and mirrored ceilings above round beds. (Aired July 1995)

We noted earlier that talk TV has much in common with game shows, and the episode of Richard Bey's program described above illustrates perfectly the game-like dimension of all such shows. Like a televised game, it has a familiar format and set, the same comforting host, competitive contestants drawn from everyday life, a studio audience, theme music, timed action, a goal, and a prize for the winner. As in the old *Queen for a Day* program, the goal is to score points as measured by the audience's reaction to what the guests reveal about themselves or others. The prizes, though less tangible than the household appliances that the Queen for a Day won back in the 1950s, are nevertheless more in keeping with our self-involved age. The guests "win" national air time for their stories of deviance, victimization, sociopathology, crime, and otherwise troubled lives. But sometimes they "win" more than they bargained for. Sometimes they also "win" the disapproval of their communities when they return home after appearing on TV. The producers of the programs "win," too, by scoring points, but their points are measured by Nielsen and Arbitron, and their winnings are cash payments through syndication, licensing fees, and the sale of commercial time.

For their part, audiences in the studio and at home are entertained, except that this particular entertainment does not come from the vicarious thrill of watching someone like themselves win money and prizes through their game skills, knowledge, or luck. It comes from watching a spectacle, a sideshow. It comes from eavesdropping on lurid and distasteful confessions. It comes from the deliberate violation of many of the rules of public demeanor that once separated the upper and middle classes from the lower class. It also comes from the co-opting of families, courts, medical therapy, and other real institutions for the purpose of creating alternative "audience-friendly" reality. In an October 1995 *Cosmopolitan* article, Marilyn Stasio asks whether audiences, in their pursuit of cheap thrills, will eventually want to see brutal violence to satisfy their bloodlust, and she quotes Amy Rosenblum, senior producer of *The Sally Jessy Raphael Show*: "I hope that people don't want this violence. . . . It was only a year ago that viewers wanted to be informed. Now they want to be entertained. There are no rules anymore, because things change so fast." Stasio adds that indeed "the guests are getting creepier and creepier, and the audiences are getting nastier and nastier" (Stasio 253). No doubt Stasio and Rosenblum are right about audience demand, but their comments are also misleading insofar as they lay the entire talk-show mess at the door of audience demand. In fact, the violators include all of the players named above: the producers of the programs, the people who appear, and those of us who listen in for our amusement.

The individuals who "competed" on Richard Bey's program openly and shamelessly told an audience of millions about their dysfunctional lives and low-class behavior. They were also encouraged by the program's producers to behave in ways that most people would still find abhorrent and humiliating, and, in turn, the audience—many of whom would not even dream of appearing on national television and making such disclosures—watched wide-eyed, snickered in amused disbelief, and looked forward to the next game of this sort. But if the contestants on the program were to be strolling through a shopping mall or occupying seats in a movie theater or sitting at our dinner table, they could not do or say the things they did on the program without social consequence—public censure, social stigma, loss of reputation, avoidance and ostracism from the group, even legal action. Nor could we laugh at their expense in public without risking some of the same social consequences or hostile confrontation with the "performers" themselves. Why, then, would each of these parties do and say things in the presence of millions of spectators that they would not do in the far more limited forum of the shopping mall or the movie theater or a host's dinner table?

The answer seems to lie in the culturally constructed frames in which all human activity operates. Once in the context of the game (or television generally, for that matter), people see themselves out of the framework of everyday life, and a whole new set of rules applies in this unreal frame. Contestants can boast about their dysfunctionality, joke about violence within the family, proudly show their cellulite, missing teeth, and tattoos, and speak inappropriately about others. For example, the obese teenager in Richard Bey's blue team says at one point that his sister's breasts are so hairy that they look like coconuts. One could hardly imagine the same statement made to strangers in the serving area of a fast-food restaurant. But the statement here merely draws an incredulous laugh, and the same kinds of strangers who, in the restaurant, would ignore him or leave in disgust, watch and encourage such talk. At the heart of all this lies a paradox: reality as we know it is suspended for the game, but this particular game (and its medium finally) is based upon what we are to assume are a real family's woes. The spectators are enticed into treating this talk like a game even though the speakers' revelations supposedly derive from their own real-life experiences. In other words, their material is drawn from one social framework and placed at the service of the game, which operates in its own context.

But because people must eventually leave the television game, it has repercussions for themselves and the viewer in the real world. Television doesn't simply reflect a segment of reality; it also changes what the audience accepts as reality. That being the case, this activity is not simply another form of play.[1] Since it changes the non-game world, it is serious, and it is dangerous. In this "spill over" effect, the talk-show "game" is analogous to commercial gambling games in which conventional games, which are meant to be "worlds unto themselves" for the sole purpose of fun, are violated since money rather than the action of play itself becomes the goal. With gambling, too, even after the game is over, there may be real repercussions in the everyday life of the players if their losses become too great not to affect their ordinary life or if they become "compulsive" players, who no longer can go from the game world back into ordinary life at will and are pathologically stuck in the play world.

The adverse social effects on one's real life of watching conflict and heightened antisocial behavior on television are well documented.[2] In his book discussing classic social-psychological studies, *Influence: How and Why People Agree to Things* (1984), for example, Robert Cialdini explains that people in groups take their behavioral cues from others. They don't define an event as an emergency or a problem when they see others doing nothing. Conversely, they are more likely to act decisively if other people in the group somehow define the significance of a situation. Applied to television, this logic explains why ludicrous laugh tracks (or "cued" laughter from a live audience) in comedies have worked so well for so long: if others are laughing, we are more prone to find the situation funny ourselves. In the same vein, if everyone on the toxic-talk program acts as if a dysfunctional family like the one featured on Bey's program is "funny" or "routine," we do, too, and eventually carry that thinking beyond the frame into reality.

Moreover, while language leads to ideas, it doesn't usually work the other way around. According to the social-psychological Whorfian Hypothesis,[3] the words we learn, hear, and speak determine how we think. It follows, then, that if misleading words are not immediately corrected, our ability to judge is adversely affected, even impaired. As we get more of our information not from direct first-hand experience with the real world but through second-hand, error-laden television talk, our ability to reason and our view of reality must suffer. Television heightens and caricatures the worst of our cultural scripts and blueprints for living with one another in the physical world. Put another way, the cyberspace of talk television undermines the real space of social reality. Confession of this sort is not good for the collective soul even if it is very good for the corporate sale.

Social order is not a given. It is not encoded in our DNA. Rather, as a species, we have developed mechanisms—laws, institutions, customs, routines, habits, etiquette—to accommodate the construction of society and social identites. Knowledge of how to behave in social situations is contained in cultural "scripts" or "blueprints" that are themselves products of human interaction and symbolic communication about the nature of reality. This "reality" differs among peoples. What is real to a Tibetan monk is different from what is real to an American businessman. While both realities may be valid within their own cultural contexts, they create in those contexts different social relationships as well as relationships with the physical world. Some cultures work better than others in dealing with the problems people face as they try to cope with one another and to survive.[4] To use a computer analogy, it's a mistake to think of our culture's view of reality as residing safely, immutably, in our collective hard drive. Rather, it is created software, and if that software is infected with a virus, it will negatively affect the workings of the cultural computer.

To keep those workings uninfected, we must curb ourselves. Morality, norms, values, and judgmental expressions of group conventions all impose limits on human behavior. In turn, these limits are maintained either by internalizing the scripts or by relying on external threats and punishments. These rules, typically the products of human agreement, provide conventional behavioral frames that allow us to act in ways that are comprehensible to all members of the group. Society is a result, then, of its boundaries, of what it will and won't allow. Shame, guilt, and embarrassment are controlling feelings that arise from doing the undoable, speaking the unspeakable—in other words, violating cultural taboos. Put another way, culture has consequences.

Moreover, social identity, governed as it is by various kinds of institutional "rules," allows us to segment reality, to look at it as we would a patchwork quilt, a whole entity whose discrete components differ significantly enough to recognize—homogeneity and heterogeneity in one fabric. We separate such activities as work and play, such experiences as the real and fictive, such behaviors that are public and private, and the stitches or constraints that hold the quilt's patches together are social norms and sanctions, the most common of which is often not imprisonment but social stigma and isolation.

Nowhere is this invention of special rules, conventions, and sanctions better visible than in games and in dramatic art (not incidentally called "plays"). In the nineteenth century, Samuel Taylor Coleridge coined the phrase "the willing suspension of disbelief" to describe the way in which we participate in fictional art. Simply explained, it means that we put on hold our understanding of how the natural/social worlds usually operate, and we suspend for a time our disbelief in such phenomena as wolves who talk and aliens from outer space. Instead, we agree to live by the special "rules" of the play. Games operate in much the same way. They occur in a special space (the game board, the field, the stage) which is at once part of and apart from real space. Time is defined not by the everyday clock but by the game or the fiction, which may allow for stopping time, extending it, or telescoping it. Rules are spelled out and agreed to in advance, and the players (and often the spectators) take on prescribed roles. The object of the game is fun, and, at the end of the play period, one is free to walk out of the frame, back to "everyday life," free of consequence. The most pervasive entertainer/information provider in our society, television, too, takes place in "unreal" space comparable to that of games and fictions, and it is viewed some thirty-eight hours per week by the average American—an astonishing amount of time to inhabit a play space. Still, if you spent thirty-eight hours a week playing Monopoly or watching baseball, what would the harm be apart from the waste of time? If you win the game or your favorite sports team loses theirs, what difference does it make to the real business of life? Not much.

What happens, though, when the game will not allow itself to be left within the artificial frame, when it spills over into everyday reality? As we've seen, such is the case with one apparent gaming activity—gambling—where addictive behavior in the "playful" atmosphere can cost people their homes, their livelihoods, even their lives. Television can be equally deceptive, equally addictive, and even more costly, especially when it shapes values, behaviors, and perceptions that we carry into everyday life. Talk television does precisely this—uses the seductive game-like frame to shape attitudes and behaviors that people take beyond the frame.

That television influences and reflects our values, that it broadcasts and disseminates a social "message," is hardly a new idea, and, again Marshall McLuhan was certainly right to argue that the medium is the message. By this he meant that any "message" will be altered by the medium through which it is communicated, that real social relationships and our experience of the world are affected by the different media to which we are exposed. The message is what the medium shows us, and that message profoundly affects the course of everyday life. There is no way to separate the changes in post-television America from the influence of television itself. Certainly there is an interaction between cultural narratives, their relative appeal, and some fifty years of television as the messenger.

Early network sitcoms like *Leave It to Beaver, Father Knows Best*, and *The Donna Reed Show* carried the "messages" that many of us wanted to hear during the 1950s, and the medium transmitted these influential messages to many middle-class households. Suburban homes with white picket fences, nuclear families with white-collar dads, domestic moms, and well-educated, well-mannered children with the same gender-based programming, two cars, summer vacations—all of these values and more were reflected in and shaped by innocent-looking television shows. By the same token, however, the mass of American viewers, particularly those in urban ghettos, did not live the way Donna and Alex Stone did. While they might admire and eventually hope to emulate the projected values, their economic and class circumstances differed considerably, and they knew it. Interestingly, in *Parenting* magazine's October 1995 issue, *Ricki Lake* executive producer Gail Steinberg defends her program on the questionable basis that *Ricki Lake* offers "a more accurate portrayal of modern-day families than sanitized fantasies like *Father Knows Best*" (21). But while neither is an accurate portrayal of complex reality, which fantasy view seems less dangerous in the long run? The earlier programs influenced desire more than they reflected the American condition. That situation would change in the decades to come as television (and its viewers) became more cynical and disillusioned.

In the sixties and seventies, the social and political messages changed, and the potent TV windows in our living rooms changed with them. The values portrayed on that screen became more liberally tolerant of diversity, less individually restrictive, and more socially proactive. (Of course, there are always exceptions. The abiding American myth of rural innocence and simplicity could still be found in shows like *The Waltons* and *Little House on the Prairie*.) Working women, minorities, single-parent households, openly declared political dissent, and generational conflict appeared in the little screen, revealing the new values of America in moral crisis. The basis of humor in *All in the Family* was a far cry from that of *Father Knows Best*, but most of us laughed just as hard because we saw our "newly aware" selves in the satiric mirror. And yet, for all their differences over time, these programs still had a number of common values, including the family and national ties that bind. Even comedies featuring grotesques like *The Munsters* and *The Addams Family* projected these values.

The eighties seemed to be a period of withdrawal from the liberal social activism of the sixties and seventies and a renewed interest in laissez-faire economics to serve private financial gain. (Again, there were exceptions, notably the enormously popular *Cosby Show*.) Along with this new emphasis on the self, the decade also brought dissolution of many common ties. The ideological battles of the conservative working-class Archie Bunker and his liberal-intellectual son-in-law Mike Stivic gave way to the selfish rudeness and socially disinterested crudeness of the Bundys in *Married . . . with Children*. Family and nation were no longer safe havens but dysfunctional and conflicted units. The message on the little screen again reflected the national message: since the social experiments and reforms of the sixties had failed to "fix" the world, the best course was to "fix" oneself, to feel good, or to escape. While many may argue that nineties "family" shows like *Home Improvement* and *Mad About You* indicate a countermovement, this pendulum theory fails to take into account the fact that the pendulum loses momentum with each swing and won't go all the way back.

Narcissism, materialism, and therapy became the avenues to personal fulfillment, and this feel-good movement ushered in an attendant decline in civic life. (This decline in civic attention, along with what Joseph Turow has called "the globalization of mass media activities" [687], has contributed to a successful push for government deregulation, a subject that we will take up later.) Armed with this therapeutic frame and the spectacular growth of the so-called "recovery movement," people substituted the idea of lasting personal character with the notion that one can remake oneself almost at will using formulas like twelve-step programs.[5] The underlying idea of this movement is that stigmatized, negatively evaluated behaviors are to be transformed into a disease frame which removes the shame, guilt, and stigma that previously acted as a container for these behaviors. What started out "I'm OK, You're OK" has become "I'm Dysfunctional and It's OK." Talk shows fit perfectly the new definition of the individual since "reputation" is no longer at stake, and its elimination liberates people to talk openly about themselves and others. On the larger scale, fixed societal rules of conduct are abandoned for an easier cultural relativity, which undermines the possibility of absolute "truth" in personal life and society.

However oversimplified this division by decade may be, it is a convenient framework for this discussion. Each decade has brought subtle changes in our society, and television is the most visible projector of these changes. The fact is that television, which has always had a symbiotic relationship with culture, has aided in the movement toward the subjective self, toward the elevation of the common person to celebrity status. In his *New York*

Times piece "The Media Monster Lurking Within" (October 17, 1995), Stephen Holden points out that, before television, there was Hollywood where larger-than-life stars lived an existence beyond us mere mortals. But when television came into our living rooms, ordinary people could be seen talking to us like our next-door neighbors. While most of us could not dream of becoming movie stars, we could easily aspire to be on television because we didn't have to be "perfect" or talented or physically attractive; the small screen cut everyone down to real-life size. Moreover, television needs round-the-clock content to be aired on network and cable outlets, and so the medium must reach further and further down for its population of characters, thus focusing its cameras upon the masses, appealing to larger amd larger audiences. "One hundred channels," writes Holden, "demanding stars for their life-and-death dramas means that 100 times as many people stand a shot at celebrity. . . . The more muddled the lines between what's real, what's half-real and what's fake, the more we sense the world as show business. And the more we groom ourselves to be video-ready for the next episode in the continuing series of our lives" (H15).

Indeed, the electronic medium has created in cyberspace (there's no *there* there!) a virtual reality that may seem more "real" than the world outside television, complete with a dysfunctional culture that fits it since there is no consequence in that nonplace and since drama still needs conflict. Why bother with real life when you could watch television's neatly packaged versions? Why bother with the responsibility of interacting with the real neighbors when you could safely watch them on TV? The activist was largely replaced in our consciousness by "the couch potato" as national vision gave way to individual voyeurism. (Baby boomers seem to have felt some guilt over their abandonment of common values, and some turned to fictional nostalgia for relief. Oldies, musical revivals, and radio stations boomed into being; *Stand by Me* did a brisk business on the big screen and *The Wonder Years* appeared on the small. But this ersatz escapist innocence was not quite convincing or hip enough to make it in the more cynical contemporary world.) McLuhan's "global village" decayed into a "place" for "global gossip," a place where we can all be "stars" in our own soap operas.

That world wanted escape *through* playing with reality, at least reality as the media served it up. Fictional communities had always existed in the mass media, all the way back to radio days. For a long time, soap operas, which originated on radio, allowed us to follow fictional characters through their "lives" in make-believe communities. However unreal those communities might be, they provided a more or less realistic fictional framework for the unfolding of the drama. But media consumers of the eighties and nineties developed a taste for "real life" entertainment with its own thrills and spills and unique surprises—so long as it was packaged correctly, that is. Truth may be stranger than fiction, but there was no reason that fiction couldn't be rendered more strange by dollops of "truth."

Absurdist drama in this century has self-consciously played with the idea of dislodged characters and social interaction. Luigi Pirandello's play *Six Characters in Search of an Author* used a double frame to take contrived characters out of one fictional context and place them into another, dramatizing the idea that there is no fixed reality, that reality itself is a subjective construction. And Edward Albee's *Who's Afraid of Virginia Woolf?* presents us with the shocking social situation of private matters blurted out to strangers (much like the talk shows). But in both cases, we are always acutely aware that what we are watching is fiction, contrived situations to make the dramatic points of the meaninglessness of life (the absurd) and the tenuousness of the social construction we call reality. Now, our media instead take real people and place them into fictional frames or bring cartoon characters to life in films. Feature films over the past decade contain many examples. *The Purple Rose of Cairo*, *The Last Action Hero*, *Sidekicks*, *Who Framed Roger Rabbit?*, *Virtuosity*, and *The Net* all blur what used to be separate realms. This trend suggests that all rules can be violated at will because there is nothing inviolate that they correspond to in reality.

Television took this "reality game" one step further since the medium and the idea that reality is simply "made up" fit together perfectly. (In fact, the connection between film and television is hardly coincidental. As we shall see later, many of the same business interests that run Hollywood also create and produce television programming.) Syndicated programs like *The People's Court*,

Emergency 911, America's Most Wanted, and *Cops* offered up real-life drama or, alternatively, dramatic views and enactments of criminal justice, while the genre known as "tabloid talk," including shows like *A Current Affair, Inside Edition,* and *Hard Copy,* extended the drama to society at large. News organizations like CNN, sensing the entertainment value of reality in this market, began continual coverage of certain hot events—the Gulf War, the William Kennedy Smith rape trial, the O. J. Simpson circus—and a two-way street developed. Television substituted its scripts for reality, and reality adopted television's techniques, finding them more entertaining than its typical ways of doing business. According to the HBO special "The Show Business of Crime and Punishment," real institutions are increasingly copying television scenarios. Attorneys emulate the in-your-face theatrics of *L. A. Law,* whose producers have said that they received many calls from real attorneys wanting copies of scripts to help them prepare for real cases! Moreover, people are now used to sitting in front of their television sets and watching baseball plays instantly replayed and enjoying the sense that the past is repeatable instantly and at will. Television talk participants are analogous in that we pay attention to one small characteristic or behavior that heightens the dramatic interest in them to the exclusion of the boring reality of their lives. In short, ominous signs already exist that virtual reality, particularly television, has begun to replace real life.

In addition to affecting our view of the unfamiliar, moreover, television and the other media have also supplanted personal experience in some cases. In a special report for *The Philadelphia Inquirer* on perceptions of crime among suburbanites (September 3, 1995), Michael Matza notes that the media's increasing coverage of violent crime has distorted people's views of actual crime rates and the potential for such crimes in the communities they inhabit. In other words, these individuals are more willing to believe media accounts than to base their behaviors on actual experience. "They are reading newspapers, magazines, and 'true crime' fiction," Matza writes, "tuning in to all news radio and watching local and network newscasts, CNN Headline News, and 'reality-based' entertainment on TV. It's a powerful combination that delivers crimes of sensational meanness straight to suburban living rooms in daily doses. . . . Sometimes the media distort reality. A survey released last year by the Center for Media and Public Affairs found that coverage of murders by the three major television networks tripled between 1992 and 1993, while the national murder rate remained unchanged" (A1, A22).

Matched with news and fictional accounts of a criminal-justice system out of control—one that supposedly lets criminals walk on technicalities and that mandates the freeing of prisoners from overcrowded jails—these carefully selected, "exciting" stories severely distort perceptions of real danger. However worrisome, these accounts are also thrilling, entertaining, akin to the fictions people watch during prime time, and that's why the news gives them so much space. Nightly newscasts overemphasize the occurrence of the deviant and the dysfunctional among us, much as talk shows do. The pictorial nature of television and the need to compete for our attention is summarized by the often quoted "If it bleeds, it leads."[6] Horrifying stories about drive-by shootings and daylight homicides unduly prompt some to worry and avoid public places, even though the likelihood that such things can happen in their own communities is small, something that experience alone can tell them. Suburban dwellers are far more likely to be victims of burglary than drive-by murder, but since the media report on the more sensational crime rather than the unexciting and pedestrian one, people believe what they are told and act accordingly, arming their homes with security systems and themselves with firearms. The media may find juicier fodder in violent crime, but people's lives are being affected by the deliberate choice of where the camera's eye is trained. The virtual version of reality is replacing actual experience.

As we have watched and marveled in ways that used to be reserved for shocking fictions, the frames that separated the real and the contrived are continually being shattered, making us less able to distinguish the public from the private, friend from stranger, and legal due process from merely the televised version of crime, trial, and punishment—in short, everything that frames our lives and gives it meaning and predictability. Although we still have to live in the actual world, we've found a way to do a lot of that living in the controlled virtual space, and in turn, we take the messages and values of the virtual entertainer through the wall into real time and place. Telecommunications replaces the barriers, restrictions, and inconveniences of real physical contact in real places (there is no weather *there*, either) with an alternative world where you can invent yourself with words "online" or on television and appear to become whoever you say you are.[7] This is the very basis of talk shows as people, out of the physical context of their real lives, construct or deconstruct themselves in front of us. In cyberspace, men can pretend to be women, the timid can masquerade as heroes, and nasty people can claim to need our sympathy and help. One of the most popular episodes of Oprah Winfrey's show featured a one-on-one interview with a woman claiming to have multiple personalities—many, many more than the literary "three faces of Eve"—and among Oprah's personal favorites was a show titled "Chucking It All," which encouraged people to leave their old lives behind and "follow their dreams." Nothing's ever final. The notion of multiple points of view or chances may be appealing but is often not an option in real life.

Curiously, the technological progress of television has not been matched by government regulation of the burgeoning medium. In fact, massive government deregulation is occurring as we write, the most dramatic recent example of which is the passage of the Telecommunications Act of 1996, which we will have more to say about in later chapters. Since the introduction of instantaneous satellite feeds, the medium has certainly changed a great deal. Fiber optics and digital compression allowed for an increase in the number of stations we could receive. This promising new and expensive technology has also led to a consolidation into a few giant entertainment cartels as Sony, Disney/ABC/Cap Cities, and Time Warner/Turner which control not one communications industry but many—magazines, recordings, films, commercial and cable television stations, distribution and syndication rights, and so on. In fact, as we shall see later, these media are concentrated in increasingly fewer hands.

Accordingly, the message that is the medium certainly changed a lot, too. Into this solipsistic wasteland came Oprah, peddling the stuff of voyeuristic dreams—"real people" airing what we assumed was their real dirty laundry in public for the nation's amusement. The "game" of television, reflective of real life but different somehow because of its inherent fictional contexts, suddenly became real, and its carefully selected slices of life became America's entertainment, effecting a perfect blurring of reality and fiction. Oprah, and later Ricki and Jenny and company, gave us a new kind of soap opera, one where the dramatic twists and turns of the fiction were replaced by shocking disclosures and where we didn't have to care about the individual characters so long as they amused us with their stories. And amuse us they do. "You're nobody if you're not on TV," the central character in the film *To Die For* says. This character is prepared to commit murder in order to be a television star. That kind of thinking has permeated modern life, especially among lower-class people, and they are willing to do anything and say anything since reputation and pride are not at risk. Being a television "star" is worth any social price.

The damaging effects of this medium on its consumers and, through them, on American society seem to us overwhelming. As we are delivered sound-bite length information presented in an entertaining "narrative" format, our attention span is shortened, and people are reduced to fictional caricatures.[8] Television's typical representation of reality is oversimplified, imagistic, out of context, brief, and easy to digest. At the same time, ironically, competition in the new global economy demands greater and more mature reasoning and analytical skills to make sense of vast amounts of information. In the age of the print medium, the development of such skills was much more likely and predictable. Books were ordered hierarchically in their levels of difficulty, and learning demanded that one had met certain prerequisites in terms of skill and knowledge in order to progress.

Does the electronic medium, notably in its presentation of talk shows, develop comparable skills in its own way? Given the medium's complexity, it ought to. Television itself is the result of complex interactions among its technical characteristics, the structure of the entertainment industry, the state of American culture, and the psychological mindset of individual viewers. But its effect on users does not match its technical, financial, and social complexity. To the contrary, its mindless pleasures demand responses that are shallow rather than profound and developed. Surface images that entertain and only remotely educate replace the kinds of detailed information provided by books and newspapers; quick emotional response replaces measured judgment about causality and consequence; passive viewing replaces active reasoning. As Tom Shachtman reiterates in *The Inarticulate Society*, clear detailed language makes a difference in our way of thinking insofar as words determine our thinking patterns rather than serving merely as vehicles. McLuhan's "the medium is the message" says precisely that. Television's images, by contrast, lead to fuzzy logic, stereotypes, and unclear distinctions. Life's complexities are thus trivialized, and our perceptions of reality altered.

In his book *Make-Believe Media: The Politics of Entertainment*, Michael Parenti notes that "the more time people spend watching television . . . the more their impressions of the world seem to resemble those of the 'make-believe media.'" Our experience of reality is affected by social forces far removed from our immediate perceptions. During the Gulf War, which some have called CNN's television war, replete with chyrons and theme music, Americans got to "participate" in antiseptic bombing raids from a safe distance. Iraq and its leaders were clearly framed as the enemy by television announcers. This was quite different from television's treatment of the Vietnam conflict in the 1960s, when we were shown different images of ourselves, and the enemy was often seen to be us. We depend on the medium's imagemakers for cues about the real world even as they invent a reality at the service of mass audiences and lucrative advertisers. Television talk shows create a different kind of war altogether. They depend upon our personal wars against our own demons, as well as the wars we wage against relatives, friends, and neighbors. In the end, however, the effect is the same as the technology of television reshapes our culture and "reality" itself.

Notes

1. For a good introduction to the classical sociology of games, play, and leisure, see Roger Caillois, *Man, Play and Games*, trans. by Meyer Barash (New York: Schocken, 1979) and Johan Huizinga, *Homo Ludens: A Study of the Play Element in Culture* (Boston: Beacon Press, 1955). For its use in the analysis of gambling games, see Erving Goffman, "Where the Action Is," in *Interaction Ritual: Essays in Face-to-Face Behavior* (New York: Anchor, 1967) and Vicki Abt et al., *The Business*

of Risk: Commercial Gambling in Mainstream America (Lawrence: University Press of Kansas, 1985).

2. For an overview of the literature on the effects of televised violence, see Aletha Huston et al., *Big World, Small Screen: The Role of Television in American Society* (Lincoln: University of Nebraska Press, 1992).

3. Benjamin Whorf, *Language, Thought, and Reality* (Cambridge: MIT Press, 1956).

4. For a discussion of this difference in "cultural capital," see Thomas Sowell, *Migrations and Cultures: A World View* (New York: Basic Books, 1996).

5. This movement has been critiqued in such books as Thomas Szasz's *The Myth of Mental Illness* (New York: Hober/Harper, 1961); Philip Rieff's *The Triumph of the Therapeutic* (New York: Harper, 1968); Stanton Peele's *The Meaning of Addiction* (Lexington, MA: Lexington/D.C. Heath, 1985) and *Diseasing of America* (New York: Lexington/Free Press, 1989); Wendy Kaminer's *I'm Dysfunctional, You're Dysfunctional* (Reading: Addison-Wesley, 1992); Charles Sykes's *A Nation of Victims* (New York: St. Martin's, 1992); and Alan Dershowitz's *The Abuse Excuse* (Boston: Little, Brown, 1995).

6. For an excellent overview of television news, see Neil Postman and Steve Powers, *How to Watch TV News* (New York: Penguin, 1992).

7. For a good analysis of this process of "morphing" on screen, see Sherry Turkle, *Life on the Screen: Identity in the Age of Internet* (New York: Simon & Schuster, 1995).

8. For a discussion of just how short the sound bite has become, see Michael Sandel's *Democracy's Discontent* (Cambridge: Harvard University Press, 1996).

3

The Star Players:
Variations on a Theme

When a contest occurs over whose treatment of the other is to prevail, each individual is engaged in providing evidence to establish a definition of himself at the expense of what can remain for the other.

—Erving Goffman
"Where the Action Is" (1967)

But the rise of capitalism over the past two centuries has meant that all the resources of technology and free enterprise could at last be placed at the disposal of the enduring human fascination with grunt and groan.

—from a *Time* magazine cover story
on the entertainment industry, June 12, 1995

We are proud to say that even in the middle of the ratings periods we've done programs on Yugoslavia. And they just didn't do well. Let's at least be honest and understand the problems of the daytime arena.

—Phil Donahue
Good Housekeeping cover story, June 1995

Jenny Jones: The game is about women who fight over guys, and Jim, Shannon, and Katrina, all of them in their early twenties, are the first set of contestants. Shannon is pregnant with Jim's child. Katrina is pregnant, too, though she won't say whether it's his baby or not. Although they've been together for six years, Katrina claims to sleep with a lot of people, so how can she know whose kid it is? Jim isn't sure either. It's possible that he's the father of Katrina's unborn child, but he knows that Shannon's is his.

Shannon is hurt by Jim's infidelities. "He just can't keep his pants zipped," she complains.

Jim dismisses her whining. He can go with any woman he wants, and it's none of her business. "My only crime is I'm treatin' women too good," he says proudly.

Katrina, who sports a half-shaven head, is also annoyed that he sleeps around, but she's tougher than Shannon. She decides to come clean, admitting that the baby she's carrying is not his, even though they're still lovers. Jim gets tough right back. "I could do her," he says. Besides, he only went with her in the first place on a bet with another guy.

That gets under Katrina's skin. She says that she put food on his table for six years. Then she softens, telling him she loves him and wants to marry him. She says it right there on TV, in front of millions of strangers. Unimpressed, he denies that they were living together at all.

Shannon still looks hurt, but a bigger hurt is waiting in the wings—a surprise guest, Jennifer, who thinks she's pregnant by Jim, too. She's brought out, and he reacts, rising to kiss her. Poor Shannon is visibly upset now.

"You're enjoying this, aren't you?" Jenny Jones asks Jim. He says something odd. They light his cigarettes, he claims, but he's not out to use them or anything. "He must have something really special," Jenny goes on, to the camera this time. "We'll take a break. We've only touched the surface."

Audience reaction shots, music, logo, commercials.

Jenny would like to go on to the next set of contestants—a woman who wants to tell her cheating boyfriend it's now or never—but first she does a recap of Jim's story. The crowd isn't quite ready to move along yet.

One audience member wonders how Jim gets these women, shouting out that he's really ugly. Somebody else tells him that he needs to grow up. Another wants to know who his next woman will be. Still another asks whether he's wearing a condom when he has sex. Jenny puts the question to him directly. No one seems to notice anymore that there are three pregnant women on stage! If he does use condoms, those women are walking advertisements for their inefficacy.

Even more bizarre is Jenny's summation statement to him. She looks at Jim, who's sitting on stage with three of his lovers, and tells him that he'll have to make a choice today. Today! (November 1994)

Although many think that the current crop of daytime talk programs claim kinship with the talk shows that began in the 1950s with Jack Paar's *Tonight Show*, the contemporary versions are actually more closely related to earlier televised games like *Queen for a Day*, *The Gong Show*, *The Dating Game*, and *The Newlywed Game*. The object of these game shows was simple—you embarrassed yourself or someone else by opening up in front of strange or supposedly familiar co-contestants, a "knowing" host who provoked tears or laughs at your expense, a studio audience, and a massive viewership. The producers of the programs made a great deal of money, and the audiences, accustomed to identifying with fictional characters in movies and sitcoms, now got a cry or a chuckle out of the embarrassingly uncontrolled patter of nonprofessional "performers," everyday people. It was like being a Peeping Tom at your neighbors' humiliations without the risk. The lure of the game for the contestants was both prizes and the chance to be on television, the latter becoming a bigger and bigger draw over time as American narcissism increased in intensity. Andy Warhol's fifteen minutes of fame, not to mention a refrigerator, could be had for a social price— a price paid by both the individual who was ridiculed and a society that learned that cruelty could be entertaining.

The familiar celebrity talk shows, most of them late-night, that began in the 1950s and continue until this day, bridged the gap between television games and talk by providing an atmosphere— the set, the familiar inquisitive host, the theme music, the live audience: the overall format—in which talk about "real" life could be carried out. But there were enormous differences between those talk shows as format exemplars and the current crop. Personalities like Jack Paar, Johnny Carson, Merv Griffin, Dick Cavett, even Phil Donahue hosted a variety hour in which public figures, professionals, came to perform and/or be interviewed. There was nothing deliberately devastating or embarrassing planned for these shows. Singers came to perform and plug new records, actors talked about new films and writers about their latest books, and politicians got some informal exposure. Rarely did everyday people appear, and when they did, it was usually done to inject some intentional humor at the end of the show, comic versions of the human-interest stories that most television-news programs sign off with. Johnny Carson might have a person who raised rattlesnakes come on and hand him a couple so that Carson could camp it up for the camera. Donahue, who met his current wife, Marlo Thomas, on one such celebrity interview on his show, often did programs on weighty and serious topics with expert guests talking about issues like free speech. Although the current hosts of late-night talk—Jay Leno, David Letterman, Conan O'Brien— have injected much more stand-up comedy into their acts, the format and subject matter remain basically intact.

The first move toward a change in the nature of the guests and the subject matter occurred in 1986, when Oprah Winfrey took a popular Chicago television program into national syndication. Like its supposed prototype, the program had a familiar host, a stage on which she sat with her guests, and a live studio audience, but that is pretty much where the similarities with talk television ended and the game-show inflence came in. Instead of interviewing famous people, this one put the spotlight on everyday folk, who got on the show not because they had a book or a film or a record or an idea to sell, not even because they had the unusual hobby of raising rattlesnakes. Rather, they got on because they were willing to reveal private matters or ease their troubled souls and possibly get "therapy" on television, in front of millions. It was the old *Queen for a Day* game show where everyday women with the most touching stories won a major appliance for being brave, desperate, or stupid enough to tell the story on television. Oprah's program differed in one major respect—there were no appliances or money as the goal. Instead, confession and dubious attention became their own rewards.

The new shows, therefore, not only merged the separate game and talk genres that had previously existed separately but they reflected the dominant values of an altered America, one that had moved beyond embracing social activism to selfish permissiveness. Strippers with large breasts went on national television to bare their souls and as much of their bodies as the censors would allow, each of these barings used to titillate and incite audiences. Men who abused women and children appeared, unflinching and shameless, rationalizing their behavior by claiming to have been victimized by society. Socially inappropriate disclosures by these guests became public matters, fair game for discussion, comment, advice, praise, and censure by the host and studio audience. The experts who appeared regularly on the prototypical talk shows had given way now to everyman and everywoman as experts on all matters.

Of course, these "experts" would have had no legitimacy, nor indeed would *Oprah* have been possible, in the decades between the first national television broadcasts (1948) and the new format's appearance in the late 1980s. By then, the national "message" had changed, and television broadcast it to the world. Since the eighties represented, at least in part, a severe reaction against the "failed" social-reform movements of the sixties, the message was simple: you can't fix complex social problems, so why even bother trying? Let's just feel good about ourselves. A marked decline in public-mindedness occurred as interest in social reform waned. Besides, feeling good didn't involve other people, only oneself; it meant becoming more self-enclosed, self-indulgent, self-improving, rude, and materialistic. Self-help books hit the shelves by the dozen, and individual "therapy" became all the rage. As social problems became exacerbated, people began to fear interaction with strangers, and so cocooning couch potatoes got off by voyeurism. Forget about spying on the neighbors. They could watch them on television.

Into this cultural vacuum came Oprah, Donahue, and Sally Jessy peddling the stuff of the armchair Peeping Tom's dreams— not the high and mighty and wealthy celebrities, performers, politicians, and intellectuals featured on *The Tonight Show*, but plain people just like them who were willing to take their actual or, more likely, their emotional clothes off in public. Watching them do so seemed safe, instructive, and a lot of fun. The game caught on quickly.

It's interesting and revealing to compare the subject matter of the three main players during one week in the early 1990s:[1]

Monday
    Oprah: Murderesses
    Donahue: Married people having affairs
    Sally Jessy: Strippers with large breasts

Tuesday
    Oprah: A woman married eight times
    Donahue: May-December relationships (couples differing
        in age)
    Sally Jessy: Feuding neighbors

Wednesday
    Oprah: Interview with Elizabeth Taylor
    Donahue: Interview with New York Governor Mario
        Cuomo
    Sally Jessy: May-December relationships

Thursday
    Oprah: Show not broadcast (*ABC After-School Special*)
    Donahue: Parents and teenaged son whose girlfriend had a
        baby
    Sally Jessy: AIDS: Epidemic or Hoax?

Friday
    Oprah: Addictive behaviors and the Betty Ford Clinic
    Donahue: Large breasts through silicon implants
    Sally Jessy: Rerun of a program on women who marry con
        artists

While this list gives us a sense of the similar subject matter, it cannot capture the differing styles of the players at the time.

By 1995, there were 18 syndicated program hosts, and a look at their subject matter during one week in August reveals remarkably little change. The only notable exception was Oprah, who considerably altered the topics and format of her program in the beginning of 1994. With her altered format, Oprah dealt more with social issues and less with personal ones:

Monday
    Oprah: The modeling industry
    Donahue: Homosexuality and crossdressing among teen-
        agers

Sally Jessy: Women jilted during pregnancy
Jenny: Matchmaking guests interested in May-December
  romances
Ricki: Women who have stolen their best friends' boyfriends
Gordon Elliott: Fulfilling a mate's romantic fantasies
Richard Bey: A date competition among women who have
  recently been dumped
Rolonda: Romantic rivalries
Maury Povich: Narrow escapes from danger recorded on
  videotape
Geraldo: The cast of *Baywatch*
Montel: Infidelity
Springer: "Springer Break '95"—reuniting spring-break
  lovers who returned home to other mates

Tuesday
Oprah: The impact of domestic violence on children
Donahue: Unusual pet stories
Sally Jessy: Abandonment by a gay spouse
Jenny: Helping children get parts in TV commercials
Ricki: Women who treat men like dirt, and the men who
  behave better the worse they are treated
Gordon Elliott: Trying to imitate a best friend (Special
  guest: Dr. Joyce Brothers)
Richard Bey: Relationship problems
Rolonda: Adult-film stars
Maury Povich: Dating
Geraldo: Teens and bisexuality (Special guest: Randy Kirk,
  author of *A Generation Betrayed*)
Montel: Followups on past guests
Springer: Meeting people who have appeared on the show
  and with whom guests fell in love

Wednesday
Oprah: TV-show families
Donahue: Parental responsibility for a child's crime
Sally Jessy: Women taking advantage of men
Jenny: Mother-daughter feuds over men
Ricki: Confronting friends about their excessive drinking
  and its effects on their relationships

Gordon Elliott: Daring a mate to do something risque
Richard Bey: Teenaged girls and sex
Rolonda: Disapproving of a teenaged relative's sexuality
Maury Povich: 900 numbers and other phone services
Geraldo: The modeling industry
Montel: Confronting one's first love
Springer: Sexy groupies girls tell all

Thursday

Oprah: Make-overs for teenagers
Donahue: Espionage
Sally Jessy: Transsexualism
Jenny: Reuniting with a former lover
Ricki: Parents who refuse to bail their children out of trouble anymore
Gordon Elliott: Reuniting with long-lost family members
Richard Bey: Confronting duplicitous friends
Rolonda: Disapproving of a roommate's romantic partner
Maury Povich: High-school reunions
Geraldo: Statutory rape
Montel: A murder case
Springer: The Great Mate Swap

Friday

Oprah: Child protection
Donahue: Assisted suicide
Sally Jessy: Incest
Jenny: Romance via computer online services
Ricki: Meeting siblings for the first time
Gordon Elliott: Guests from previous programs
Richard Bey: Confronting an unfaithful mate
Rolonda: Men who father children with numerous women
Maury Povich: Favoritism in families
Geraldo: Unruly teens
Montel: Disapproving of a child's attire
Springer: (Not broadcast on Fridays)

Of the 59 topics listed, the majority are about a handful of topics: dysfunctional families, dysfunctional sexuality, troubled romance, or troubled teenagers and their troubled mothers, and invited or unwanted reunions. Oprah's topics ran the gamut from the innocuous (the modeling industry) to the serious (children and domestic violence). As always, Donahue tried to balance the ticket, covering the serious topics he preferred like assisted suicide and typical talk-show fodder like crossdressing in the same week. Geraldo has said he would follow suit, but he is still associated with sleazy topics, at least on his syndicated talk show. (His cable program on CNBC is another matter, as we have seen.) The others are virtually alike in topic, and there is considerable overlapping. Of the 59 topics, four (7%) might be considered serious or socially useful (e.g., assisted suicide, children and domestic violence), 9 (15%) innocuous (e.g., pet stories, high-school reunions), and a whopping 46 (78%) are about sex, behavioral disturbances, and families out of control.

Just as disturbing as the subjects themselves is the manner in which they are solicited. Most of the programs feature toll-free numbers that viewers can call if they have topics that might interest the producers. Of course, those topics must accord with the general tenor of the program, hence the self-perpetuating nature of the stories. Sometimes, the invitations to participate are very specific, with voice-overs by the hosts themselves. "If your daughter's too much of a party girl and you want to confront her about her wild lifestyle, call . . ." went one spot on a recent *Maury Povich Show*. "If you're a teenaged girl who wants to reveal a sexual secret to your mom, call . . . ," Jenny Jones requests on another. Often, advertising space is purchased in print media, and occasionally even "informational" pieces appear in popular magazines. The September 1995 issue of *Good Housekeeping*, for example, contained articles about appearing on game shows and talk shows. The latter piece begins, "If you've got a great story to tell, a gripping tale of passion or betrayal, or you simply hunger for a makeover, you just might have a shot at being a guest on a talk show." It goes on to describe the topics considered promising for a few of the shows. Ricki and Jenny, we're told, invite stories about "reuniting people." Among the most popular topics of the genre, segments on "reunions" generally feature close-ups of teary-eyed guests in the most intimate of emotional moments. These guests are then asked to tell the audience how they feel over seeing a long-lost lover or sibling or child or parent.

The fact of the matter is that these programs are very much alike in format and substance because television itself is a very derivative medium. A network looks for an idea that works, and the others copy it. On the other hand, the styles of the players must differ markedly if the game is to appear "original," and those that are too imitative (e.g., Rolonda trying to be like Oprah) are generally less successful. Nevertheless they all communicate "accessibility." None is too demanding of the studio audience, and all communicate the assumption that no one is superior to anyone else. None is too intellectual or elitist, and to one degree or another, all are quick at the glib, superficial response, which all but ignores the variability of the human condition. From the beginning to the present, all of the successful programs feature players who are brilliant performers, making what they do look easy and projecting styles that are both distinctive and familiar.

Oprah

The foremost of the talk-show hosts, actress Oprah Winfrey, turned a local Chicago program into a nationally syndicated show in 1986, a show that quickly became the standard for all such programs. The winning combination of real, "everyday" guests, provocative topics and formats, and a professionally honed caring and informal style made Oprah a media celebrity. Ten years, and many Emmys, later, *TV Guide*'s January 4-7, 1997, issue, which features a photo of a glamorous Oprah on its cover, named her "Performer of the Year."

Curiously, however, her fabulous fame and fortune seem to be at odds with the everyday-folk persona that she projects on television, but to her audience, she is the embodiment of the latter-day American Dream—the poor girl who worked hard, got straight A's in school, overcame the obstacles of racial prejudice, obesity, sexual abuse as a child, and crack-cocaine use as an adult, and became one of the most famous women in the world. Despite her good fortune, however, she maintains behavioral ties to her "roots," projecting a sense of being everyone's friend; that kind of behavior is important to viewer identification with her. Working-class and middle-class Americans love a winner because he or she holds out hope for what they can become if they work at it, but nobody loves a snob who turns away from their humble origins.

Through her frequent use of colloquial diction, occasional physical contact with guests and audience, and down-to-earth humor, she can appear both common and special, at once part of and apart from the masses.[2]

In the same vein, although she was the pioneer of the TV confessional game, her treatment of guests is far gentler than that of her competition. Although she is occasionally sarcastic, her offhand remarks are less biting than teasing, and she rarely makes fun of her guests or uses them as objects of ridicule. Instead, Oprah projects a sense of caring and compassion, as she freely gives advice. In the earlier shows, she would spend a whole hour with one guest, sitting on stage beside him or her in what appeared to be a supportive role. Over time, as the advent of new programs lit a fire under the ratings competition, she took her place with the audience and left guests isolated and unprotected. (In her latest transformation, however, she again often sits with the guests and even touches them encouragingly.)

Still, she remains in a class by herself, and as of this writing, she continues to maintain the number-one ratings position, although her recent change to less scandalous subjects and format has cost her ratings points in addition to those she lost in 1993 to her competitors, notably Jenny Jones and Ricki Lake. According to the October 10, 1994, issue of *Variety*, her 52-week average had already decreased from a 10 rating in the 1992-1993 season to a 9.2 rating during the 1993-1994 season. Moreover, her ratings for the first three weeks in 1994-1995 were down by 18% compared to that period in 1993-1994.

Her show is now primarily about her own persona, the decision to take the high road brought about by her unwillingness and/or inability to compete with the down-and-dirty Jenny Jones and Ricki Lake. Because of the ratings slippage that had already begun to occur, both "The Shameless World of Phil, Sally and Oprah" and Vicki Abt's appearance on Oprah's program at the beginning of the 1994 season seem to have had a lot to do with her decision to move away from trashy talk. If Oprah was looking for an excuse to change, she found it in this work. The 1995 season opener even began with a disclaimer disavowing the "trash" being put on the air by her competitors.

These days her topics are more middle-of-the-road, and she often features middle-class people as guests. Topics range from the common problem of finding trustworthy and reliable childcare providers to fawning celebrity interviews[3] to large social problems like the effects of violence on the family. Occasionally, however, she flirts with the "old" format, doing shows on topics like female circumcision. Another of her recent additions is a feature called "Oprah's Bookclub," which makes instant hits and bestsellers for a few fortunate titles. The books chosen are usually "uplifting," though few of them are seriously critical of the culture that supports Oprah. Regardless of her subject matter, however, Oprah herself is doing fine financially. According to *Forbes* magazine's September 1995 issue, she was the second-highest-paid entertainer in America (after Steven Spielberg), with an income in 1994 of about $146 million.

Donahue

We include a description of Phil Donahue despite his retirement from the talk-show business since it was he who introduced the world to the audience-participation element of the genre some 29 years ago. Although a veteran of TV talk programs, Phil Donahue seemed the least comfortable in his newer role in recent years as scandalmonger. A liberal intellectual and the author of *The Human Animal* (1985), Donahue distanced himself from his guests and audiences, and his comments were often acerbic, pedantic, sarcastic, or cynical. Although their topics were similar, even overlapping at times, he was very different stylistically from Oprah.

Unlike Oprah, who uses colloquialisms and other speech adjustments to make herself homey and accessible to the audience, Donahue often resorted to cold exclamations like *alas* and employed verbal irony at every turn. On one program, for instance, a guest said something particularly shocking, and the host turned to the audience with a deadpan look on his face and said, "You wanted to know." On a show about feuding engaged couples, he looked into the camera and said of the rowdy studio audience, "Here's another judgmental New York audience," and then he said to the guests, "Hope you're registered at Bloomies." Also unlike Oprah, he rarely gave advice or offered "useful" feedback, taking on the role of exposer rather than that of therapist or friend.

As indicated in the quote by Donahue at the beginning of this chapter, he seemed to prefer serious topics to scandal, but he also well understood what drove the ratings. In the September 24, 1995, magazine section of *The Philadelphia Inquirer*, Stephen Seplow quotes Donahue in an about-face, since retirement, lauding talk shows that deal with these forays into the personal lives of the masses: "The more we see people courageously healing, confronting their past and talking about it openly in a public forum, the less likely it is that someone is going to abuse your baby sister or mine or anyone else's" (14). However, Donahue failed to explain why it is that domestic abuse, homicides, teen pregnancies, and other indicators of social pathology have actually increased in the years since Oprah popularized this transformation in the talk-show genre.

Still, Donahue occasionally did a program on a current news event like the ones he did on the House banking scandal a few years ago, but until recently he had managed to hold his own in the more lurid world that appeals to viewers. But, toward the end, his ratings slipped dramatically as he tried to compete with younger hosts and their more scandalous topics and formats. In fact, by his last season, he'd lost his outlets in two top-five markets—New York and San Francisco—and in the fourth-rated Philadelphia market, he lost his 9 A.M. slot to Maury Povich. On the other hand, however, according to the August 21, 1995, issue of *New York* magazine, he nevertheless did very well financially. His syndicator, Multimedia, in which he was a major stockholder, was sold to Gannett for $1.7 billion, and Donahue himself received a multi-million-dollar profit from the deal.

Sally Jessy

Sally Jessy Raphael is the most stylistically interesting though the least dramatically riveting of the three early prototypes. Unlike Oprah and Donahue, who project distinctive and imposing personalities on their programs, Sally's persona is almost nonexistent. She acts as if she, like the audience, is there just to listen, observe, and occasionally comment. She does not distance herself from the audience or the guests in any significant sense. It's a brilliant disguise. She too is the consummate professional, having started on radio at the age of twelve, and her present talk show started in 1982. Deliberately subordinating her own star status to the guests and their subject matter, she appears so homey, intimate, and non-threatening that she can get guests to admit things they might not to the superstar Oprah or the distant and forbidding Donahue. (In fact, Sally took over the slot that used to be occupied by Donahue when he lost his New York outlet in August 1995. Then, in January 1997, she was moved to the slot opposite Oprah herself and the newer *Montel Williams Show*.)

Sally's program focuses on the guests, and, of the three hosts, her identification with the audience is the most complete, in diametric opposition to Donahue's uneasy relationship with his guests and audience. Some of the tactics that she uses to get guests to open up to her are silly but effective. Exuding a sense of concern and caring at all times, she'll say such things as, "Just between you and me, what happened?" Few if any stop to question the fact that this particular "you and me" disclosure has millions of eavesdroppers listening in. Although she does not appear deliberately sarcastic when she makes such remarks, she is being deceptive, preying upon people who are disoriented by the strangeness of the television production process (at which Sally is a pro, of course), flattered by the audience's attention, and taken in by the expert show of concern by the host. *New York Times* editorialist Bob Herbert, on February 26, 1996, wrote a brilliantly descriptive piece on *The Sally Jessy Raphael Show* called, appropriately enough, "Double Exploitation." In the article he writes of his experience watching one of the shows:

For those who find enjoyment, excitement and lots of laughs in the sexual exploitation of children, I offer you the Sally Jessy Raphael experience. I had the misfortune to see last Monday's show which was titled "My Teen Can't Go Without Sex." It was like spending an hour in an unclean bathroom. The show opened with several comments like the following: "Sally, my little girl is only 12 years old, but she's already had sex with 25 guys!" Loud prurient cheers erupted from the studio audience and the music intensified as Ms. Raphael kicked off a show that was unrelentingly vile and degrading, and brutally abusive to its young guests. The girls (no boys) were encouraged, cajoled and all but coerced into revealing excruciating details of their promiscuity. They were then roundly denounced, cursed, reviled, laughed at and otherwise humiliated by the rowdy audience. They were even chastised by Ms. Raphael, an empty-headed and maddeningly self-righteous host. . . . The children on Ms. Raphael's show . . . were betrayed. By definition, they were excessively needy. That is the case with all sexually exploited children. But instead of getting help from a powerful authority figure like the host of a nationally syndicated television show, these children were brutally victimized again. The abuse was not limited to the young. The mother of the 12-year-old seemed to be mentally retarded. When she made a tearful comment that was uttered with difficulty and was grammatically incorrect, the audience and Ms. Raphael broke into uncontrollable laughter. The daughter, distressed, looked on helplessly. What fun. (A13)

We've quoted this piece at length because it so perfectly captures the nature of this so-called helpful entertainment.

In point of fact, Sally rarely gives confrontational advice or on-air therapy. A recent segment titled "I'm Marrying a 14-Year-Old" featured a thirty-one-year-old woman who had a son the same age as her fiancé. (Her three children, incidentally, are not living with her but with her alcoholic and abusive ex-husband.) While the audience openly expresses disapproval of the woman and her revelations, Sally implores them to "let her talk" and suggests that "maybe we're being a little hard on Lisa." To keep the fifteen-minute segment from breaking up, Sally tries to appear professionally casual about this obvious case of child molestation. "Aren't we being a bit strong?" she asks the audience, which, fortunately, disagrees completely.

Sally differs from Oprah and Donahue in other significant ways as well. Whereas the other two often come prepared with some notecards from which they can cite statistics and other information to guests, Sally appears the least knowledgeable about the guests' subjects, preferring to let discussion flow from the evolving confession. At other times, though, we've noticed that there isn't enough discussion and far too much tawdry exhibition. One program featured a philosophical pimp, who said, "People come to me looking for a way out, okay?" No one, least of all Sally, saw fit to say that it was *not* okay! And in a September 1995 program on a mother who can't control her sixth-grade daughter's sexuality, the "caring" Sally encouraged the young girl to show the audience the dance that she had done in front of a group of boys. Dressed in a short, skin-tight black dress, the girl gyrates sensually in front of her distressed mother, the studio audience, and the world at large.

In ironic contrast to her ability to get others to open up, Sally says almost nothing on the air about her own personal life or lack of successful experience with her own family's personal problems. Until her daughter's suicide some years ago, there was practically no newspaper, magazine, and tabloid (print and TV) coverage of this talk superstar, whereas Oprah is a fixture, and Phil's celebrated marriage to Marlo Thomas gets press in places like *Good Housekeeping* (see the June 1995 cover story). Curiously, when Sally did eventually decide to talk on the air about her daughter's death, the message she read was short and unintentionally ironic. "I made a decision long ago," she said, "that, although this was the way I made a living, I would never put her in the spotlight. Allison didn't want it. She was a very private person."

This statement, which is undoubtedly true, may also be as deceptive as the tactics she uses to get people to talk, especially in view of its context and timing—she said it in the course of a program about incest survivors. One is left to wonder whether it was all right to air ugly details about other people's troubled kids while sheltering her own children and hiding her own tragedies. After all, if something useful to society is to be learned from disclosures about incest, isn't there an even more valuable lesson lurking in a story about the potentially more pervasive problems of drug abuse and suicide? Some (like Bob Herbert) might call this hypocrisy in action.

Geraldo

Geraldo Rivera, an attorney and former New York television news reporter, represents a transitional figure who took the style, format, and subject matter of the prototypes and brought them down to new lows. In this way, he is both "heir" to the revolution that Oprah started and the "father" to the more shocking performers turned talkers turned sideshow entertainers that followed. Whereas Oprah, Donahue, and Sally Jessy tended to hide their shameless probing behind the curtain of socially "useful" talk, Geraldo was responsible for the first tatters in the curtain, revealing the thing itself—deviance played strictly for shocks. By the time we get to the new kids on the block, the curtain is often discarded completely.

No stranger to tabloid television, Geraldo is famous for airing programs like the opening of Al Capone's vault on live television. (Capone was no doubt smarter than the host, the producers, and especially the audience. The vault contained nothing.) Geraldo is also famous because of his coverage *by* the media. The disclosure in his autobiography of his having had sex backstage with a number of the celebrity guests who appeared on his program made tabloid and news headlines.[4] That proud boast of his sexual prowess, which embarrassed many of the actresses who were named, reveals a lot about Geraldo's style not only in the way he lives his life, but also how he conducts his talk program.

Boisterous, aggressive, and utterly shameless in his probing questions, Geraldo goes out of his way to incite both his guests and the studio audience. Not surprisingly, his program has been known to erupt in unplanned physical violence during taping sessions, and the producers made sure that this titillating show of real-life violence wasn't left on the cutting-room floor. Members of racist and other hate groups appear on his show with regularity, and on one program, aired in 1994, Geraldo used the term "Jew York" to mock and incite his Skinhead guests. (His disclaimer that he himself was half Jewish was supposed to make this provocative epithet acceptable.) In another program during the 1995 season, his idea of "help" to lower-class gang girls was to give them a make-over. (What about giving them a cultural make-over, including lessons in English, attitude, deportment, and so on?) Recently, he turned his attention to that pressing and pervasive social phenomenon "Kids Who Kill Their Parents." He has done similar programs in the past, and so have other talk-show hosts. Given the amount of time spent on this bizarre subject, in fact, one might get the impression—and many viewers do—that such homicides have reached epidemic proportions, and they have not. This is a classic example of the ways in which talk shows distort reality, and Geraldo is among the worst offenders in this regard.

There are few boundaries that Geraldo will not cross, even though he often claims on the air that he respects such boundaries. A 1995 program provided a good case in point. The show, which was titled "When Stepfathers Step Over the Line," was about girls molested and made pregnant by their stepfathers. In one segment, a young daughter was reunited with her biological father after she gave birth to a child fathered by her stepfather. Unintentionally ironic was Geraldo's saying to the man present, "I don't want to overstep my bounds," as if any of this tragic business being broadcast to millions was within the bounds of normality. Then he asked the man, "Do you want to touch your granddaughter?" The granddaughter in question, the result of the boundary-shattering relationship between daughter and stepfather, was sitting on her mother's lap. Geraldo and his producers surely crossed some line with this lurid program (one among many), and so did those of us who watched and listened.

To say the least, Oprah, Donahue, and Sally Jessy appear mild by comparison to Geraldo in his syndicated-talk persona. Interestingly, his persona on his cable-television program on CNBC is radically different from the one he displays on his toxic-talk show. The CNBC show is more serious in subject, intelligent in approach, nonexploitative of his guests, and dealing with social and political issues. Asked by *TV Guide* in its August 26–September 1, 1995, issue how he felt about being a "showman" by day and a serious news analyst by night, Geraldo responded, "Critics seem to revel in pointing out the inconsistency of being both things. I'm *glad* I have both. Prior to the CNBC program, I felt I was using only half of my brain." Of course, this implicit acknowledgment of his two personas just goes to show that these performers will do whatever the market demands. Just six months after the *TV Guide* issue came out, *The Philadelphia Inquirer*, in an article entitled "Geraldo Rivera Says Ratings Drop Won't Run Him off the High Road" wrote, "Geraldo Rivera once got his nose broken during a brawl on his show. But lately, he says, his tabloid daytime show has made him want 'to slit my throat when I shaved in the morning'" (Shister C8). Which high road? Which Rivera? "In life, in fiction, in politics, it's now 'reinvent,' 'revise' and 'redefine,'" writes *New York Times* commentator Michiko Kakutani in a particularly telling critique of our age (C11). Geraldo illustrates this tendency perfectly.

Jenny

Notoriety is the spice of life on talk television, and real-life scandal can help capture some ground in the ratings wars. During a March 1995 taping of a program featuring people who had secret crushes on acquaintances, Jenny Jones, stand-up comic turned talk-show host, brought about the public discovery of one such crush—the one that Scott Amedure, a 32-year-old gay man, had on his straight friend, Jonathan Schmitz, 24. A little while after this humiliating encounter, Schmitz reportedly went to Amedure's home and murdered him. Although the program was never aired, the incident made international headlines and had a more dramatic effect than showing it could ever have brought about—soaring ratings at the time.

Jenny differs in small ways from her major competitor, Ricki Lake. While Ricki greets guests' startling revelations with a kind of wide-eyed wonder, Jenny is very serious. Ricki also appears to be an innocent, reacting to all of this confession with as much shock and concern as her audience, whereas Jenny looks experienced and impassive. Although both invite the audience to be critical and participatory, Jenny's control of the "fiction" is smoother than that of her younger counterpart, and she is much less likely than Ricki to break frame with asides and other seemingly spontaneous behavior.

As an ironic footnote to the murder case involving the Jenny Jones show, a supermarket tabloid ran a story in April of 1995 titled "Jenny Jones Gets Round-the-Clock Guard After Death Threats." These threats were supposedly leveled by people who blamed her for Amedure's death. According to an "insider" at the program, "Many of these angry folks unfairly charge that Jenny ultimately caused an innocent man's death in her pursuit of higher ratings." Other insiders claimed that Jenny "is devastated to find that many viewers blame her for staging the show that led to the slaying." She was apparently not devastated enough by the act itself, however, to take any blame for inciting it, as her subsequent trial testimony revealed, nor did her devastation cause her to rethink the subject matter of the show or whether the show was worth producing at all. In August 1995, the New York *Daily News* reported that Jenny Jones had been named in a $25 million lawsuit on behalf of Amedure's family.

Ironically, too, the Jenny Jones murder case spawned a copy-cat in Rolonda, who later aired a similar "outing" of secret loves on her program in her own quest for higher ratings. This segment was featured within a week of Rolonda's appearance with Vicki Abt on *The Today Show* (March 3, 1995) discussing the Amedure murder. Both in discussion in the green room and on the air, Rolonda agreed that this kind of program was dangerous and irresponsible and argued that her program was "different." So much for the differences. (Ironically, the same month of the Amedure taping, a supermarket tabloid featured a light article about Jenny's fear of flying in a plane and another one about Rolonda's dating six men at the same time. There they were again, two competing talk-show stars in the same gossipy tabloid.) And, as if that murder and Rolonda's repeating the circumstances that provoked it weren't enough, Ricki Lake did a show in the 1995 season in which women and men who had fallen in love with previous guests on the Ricki show would have a chance to meet and woo the objects of their passion.

Ricki

The most successful of the newer players, actress Ricki Lake, in 1995 occupied the number-two ratings slot and had been quickly gaining on her main competitor, Oprah. In fact, Sony Pictures Entertainment even created an Internet home page for Ricki, replete with a promo and hypertext buttons that led to photos of Ricki, audio and video clips of the show, bios of the star and the program's producers, upcoming show topics, and a news item on how Ricki was selected to host the show and proceeded to "turn on a generation."[5]

That "generation," according to the promo, is the younger, MTV set—the very people who are high-tech enough to find this sophisticated ad on the World Wide Web and who have made her number two in what the copy terms the "daytime talk wars." To these younger people, it makes a couple of deliciously tempting promises: that Ricki will let them "eavesdrop on other people's traumas and dramas in a cutting edge daytime forum designed to keep action hot and audience members involved," and that Ricki's "trademark compassion, intellect, and irresistible charms creates [*sic*] an atmosphere where guests and audience members feel comfortable letting it all hang out with absolute candor and some surprising results."

Like many other talk-show hosts, Ricki Lake is an actress. She has appeared in nine feature films, in one television movie, and in a recurring role on the ABC program *China Beach*. That fact may add to her celebrity appeal and bring in the younger viewers, but it also subtly ensures that "people's dramas and traumas" will be played out theatrically and with a new twist: this "theater" will feature one charming professional actress playing at wonder and concern and many amateurs playing with their own lives and reputations for other people's amusement. It is also common knowledge among insiders that the apparent spontaneity of her reactions is actually a performance. She reportedly wears a small listening device through which the producers "call the plays."

And what subject matter does Ricki offer for their amusement? One "amusing" subject involved some obese people who wanted to lose weight but remain fat to keep their mates and the "therapist" who will help these people "find their own happiness." Such therapists, incidentally, are a common fixture on the newer talk shows, and Ricki has featured the most famous of these fixtures, Dr. Joyce Brothers. The celebrity pop psychologist, who gained fame during her stint as a "boxing expert" on the old *$64,000 Question* show, stood in a booth on the program and dispensed one-minute therapy to guests who were "referred" to her by Ricki. Of course, we got to overhear everything that took place in these therapeutic sessions. Another of Ricki's recent "amusing" topics was "I Know I'm Ugly . . . But I Can Get Anyone I Want." The sideshow curiosities of circuses in the past—the 600-pound fat man, the bearded lady, the midget—have nothing on their latter-day electronic counterparts.

Some Other Players and the Shape of Things to Come
Other players in this crowded game field include Montel Williams, Richard Bey, Jerry Springer, Maury Povich, and Gordon Elliott. Like their previously described competitors, they represent variations on a theme, similar in format and substance, but different in style and approach.

Montel's modus operandi resembles Geraldo's, but if possible he is even more aggressive and judgmental toward the guests, and he incites more direct audience participation. A former military man and "motivational speaker," he is also not shy about giving "therapy" to his guests—virtually all of it simplistic and, therefore, virtually useless. He might tell a troubled teen to listen to his parents while giving the same advice about listening to the teen's parents. Also, contradictions abound. In one recent program about mothers who invade their daughters' privacy, he read on the air from a girl's diary, revealing publicly the very things she wished to hide from her mother, not to mention from the world. In a June 1996 show devoted to showcasing "Women Who've Survived Tragedy," Montel, in a particularly egregious display of psychobabble, "explained" to the women guests that telling the gruesome details of how it felt to be shot, knifed, or otherwise abused to millions of strangers—Montel's home audience—was, indeed, necessary for their "working through" their pain. Of course this was a distortion of the presumed benefits of talking about one's traumas, in privacy, to trusted counselors or professionals, in controlled settings under conditions constrained by appropriate protocols designed to keep further traumatization at a minimum. A television show's ratings don't figure in the equation during the "healing" process, which may take years to occur, if ever.

The clown prince of the talk-show realm, Richard Bey (currently on hiatus from taping new shows) often plays the guests and the audience for laughs and does oddball things. He once invited some blindfolded men to see if they could identify their wives or girlfriends by touch alone, and in another stunt, he had women put their breasts through holes in a board and had the audience throw cream pies at them. Like Ricki, he also offers his guests one-minute therapy, but with a comical twist. On one program, frequent talk-show "therapist" Dr. Judy Kuriansky (or "Dr. Judy," as he calls her) donned a 1950s roller-skating outfit and skated up to offer "in-your-face" therapy to the guests. In another recent program, she dressed as Catwoman, presumably in tribute to the latest *Batman* release. If these stunts do not represent the ultimate mockery of real therapeutic help, we don't know what does.

Springer, the former mayor of Cincinnati is among the most shameless of this group. Sex figures prominently in Springer's show. One 1995 program was titled "The Great Mate Swap," featuring couples who decide to exchange mates for an evening to see what it's like. One set of contestants, composed of two sisters and their boyfriends, are set up in a motel, and Springer's cameras are there to capture the pre-swap festivities. One couple is dressed only in bath towels, and as romantic music plays in the background, the heavily tattooed man is seen solicitously offering his mate's sister champagne and pouring bath oil in the tub in preparation for their bath together. (Of course, all of this leads us to question just how much of this is staged spectacle as opposed to spontaneous revelation—which many programs promise.) In September of 1995, Springer reaired a segment that was particularly illustrative of his sanctimonious and cynical style. A mother collapses after being screamed at by her transvestite drag queen son and straight daughter. The cameras continue to roll as the mother is placed on a stretcher, and as she is being wheeled away to a waiting ambulance, Springer is seen holding her hand and wiping her brow. Of course, his "concern" is questionable, particularly in light of his reairing the program. Finally, in still another 1995 program entitled "Club Kids," Springer featured ten transvestites with names like Queer Donna and Vendetta Slut. At one point, he brings out Queer Donna's aunt, who expresses concern for the man's safety and orders him to take off his ridiculous outfit, which is patterned in Madonna's style—hence the punning name. Queer Donna, who is exceptionally obese, mockingly agrees and begins to do a striptease, at which time Springer, laughing uproariously, turns to his audience and asks, "What's wrong with me?" Did he really have to ask? Does he really want to know? Appearing with Abt on a CBS *This Morning* segment (November 1, 1995) about William Bennett's attack on talk shows, Springer shrugged off the matter of the talk shows' inappropriate topics as "just entertainment."

Although Maury Povich is a long-time journalist and a television talk-show host with a Philadelphia-based program, he, too, has decided to cash in on the syndicated talk craze, and so, along with his cohorts, he daily plumbs the toxic depths. In a 1995 program titled "Forgiving the Unforgivable," he unites victims and their attackers, urging the victims to make peace with those who hurt them by understanding "where the attacker was coming from." One such attacker was "coming from" a life in the ghetto, but then again, so was his victim, a teacher who was coaching a team when he was violently assaulted, causing him to lose an eye and to have a plate inserted into his skull. The assault is even captured on tape, which is shown during the program. At the end, Maury congratulates the attackers for having the "courage" to come on and face their victims. Of course, these same individuals had the "courage" to perform horribly violent acts, and now they are commended for having more strength of character. On the other hand, the victims are expected to accept the apologies of those who have injured them, and those who would hold a grudge and won't forgive are deemed somehow deficient. To say the least, this show and others like it represent the world turned upside down. Maury's most bizarre show, however, dealt with anorexic twins, one of whom was in the studio dressed as scantily as possible to show off her skeletal condition. Immediately following her plea to the audience not to go on "crash diets," a commercial for quick weight loss was aired.

The baby-faced Charles Perez seemed to be gaining ground until his show ceased production in 1996. His program, however, amply illustrated all of the oversimplifications, deceptions, and manipulations of the talk shows that we consider throughout this book. In a program at the start of the 1995 season, he featured a group of "Momma's Boys," very young men whose mates complained that their "men" were too attached to and dependent upon their mothers. In most cases, the "men," some of them the fathers of children, appeared to be well below average in intelligence, and their realistic prospects of their supporting these women in the independent style they demanded were nonexistent. In other words, it was no great surprise or revelation that they were "momma's boys"; it was perfectly clear that their intellectual and emotional levels were those of ten-year-olds, even if their physical maturity allowed them to make babies, and that the women to whom they were married or mated (most of them older than the "men") were unrealistic in their expectations. Nevertheless, the rowdy audience (most of them visibly no better in class or condition than the guests), the "concerned" host, and his "therapist," Dr. Gilda Carle, offered mindless panaceas that would help the couples live happily ever after *sans* mother. (Carle, incidentally, appears from time to time on various shows using various titles. On the Perez show, which was aired during the early 1995 season, she was indentifed as a "psychotherapist," but when she was featured on Richard Bey's show the following week, she was identified as "The Love Doc" for MTV OnLine.) The entire display was embarrassing, socially useless, and deliberately mean-spirited.

Regrettably, as we noted earlier, the toxic waste site called talk television is hardly about to be closed down. New shows are churned out each season, even though most of them will not be continued beyond that single season. More troubling than the proliferation of programs, however, is the fact that fewer than ten companies now control all of these widely syndicated market segments, along with other major entertainment media. The dangers of concentrating such programming in fewer and fewer corporate hands is a subject that we will take up in chapters 6 and 7. Before we can consider the matter of media ownership, we need to look at the rules of this deceptive talking game.

Notes

1. In a study for the Kaiser Family Foundation, "The Content of Television Talk Shows," researchers at Michigan State University report the following ratings points for the top ten talk shows in December 1994, with each point representing approximately one million viewers: 1) Oprah—8.9; 2) Ricki Lake—5.3; 3) Jenny Jones—4.3; 4) Sally Jessy—4.2; 5) Maury Povich—4.0; 6) Montel— 3.8; 7) Phil Donahue— 3.6; 8) Geraldo—3.2; 9) Jerry Springer—2.5; and 10) Gordon Elliott— 2.4.

2. Abt's experience taping the show adds credence to Oprah's abilities to put people at ease before and during the show. Her first question to Abt, off-camera, was, "How do you like my shoes?" referring to her new, very fashionable footware. It was as if they were old friends, and Abt's fashion opinion counted for something. During the course of the show, Oprah continually referred to Dr. Abt as "Vicki," and, even when the audience was furious at Abt for attacking talk shows and especially their icon, Oprah Winfrey, Oprah acted as if she would protect her guest while evoking argument and negative responses from the audience by the loaded questions. Never did Oprah go directly against audience opin-

ion (though, between the time of that show and today, she has adopted almost every suggestion Abt made which Oprah then opposed and laughed at). Through it all, Oprah's charisma was overwhelming. It was difficult not to believe in her sincerity and good will. She would make the perfect government diplomat.

3. Oprah plays the role of everyman/everywoman in her childlike awe and excitement over meeting pop celebrities. For example, in her January 1997 interview with John Travolta and some of the stars in his new hit movie *Michael*, she told the actor and the audience how thrilled she was that she actually got a chance to touch him. That she was at least as famous as Travolta was not evidenced in the proceedings. Her exaggeration of the importance of her celebrity guests was also apparent in a show on basketball star Michael Jordan. "Just about the most famous man on the planet is here," she gushed as she began the show.

4. In an understated documentation of top-rated talk-show interactions, researchers at Michigan State University prepared a report for the Kaiser Family Foundation concluding that Geraldo Rivera's daytime talk show had the "highest average number of criminal disclosures" (six) and that "abuse" was more often discussed on his show than any other.

5. Airport bookstores and similar outlets of easy reading paperbacks for the mass audience have several offerings billed "bios" of top talk-show hosts, their titles typically being the first name of the host. Examples include *Ricki!* by Robert Waldron (New York: Boulevard Books, 1995) and *Oprah!* by Nellie Bly (New York: Zebra Books, 1993). These are little more than "puff" pieces by authors who have also written bios on other talk-show celebrities. Suffice it to say that depth or contradictions to the celebs' own "spin" factories won't appear between the covers of the books. Some talk-show hosts have even written their own accounts of their lives. Montel Williams's autobiography is aptly titled *Mountain, Get Out of My Way* (New York: TWAB, 1995), and Oprah's autobiography awaits her newly published cookbook, written with her former cook, now a celebrity writing her own memoirs.

4

Entertaining Sin:
The Rules of the Game

Self-restraint seems almost sacrilege in a society that depends
on the dogma of economic materialism . . . [t]he excitement of
demands for more . . . and the almost infinite extension of the
market. . . . Instead of [materialism] being regarded as a means
to an end . . . it has become the supreme end of individuals and
society alike. . . . Thereupon the appetites thus excited have
become freed of any limiting authority.

—Emile Durkheim,
Suicide (1897)

A society that insists on stressing self-expression over self-
control generally gets exactly what it deserves.

—Charles Sykes,
A Nation of Victims (1992)

Who needs meaning, after all, if you can have constant sensation? . . . Thinking limits one's commercial possibilities.

—Tom Grimes,
City of God (1995)

*Montel: The music is uncharacteristically slow and serious to fit
the gravity of the subject: the reunion of mothers and their run-
away teenaged daughters. Like the theme music added to movies
it's there to put the audience in the right frame of mind, to set the
tone and mood, but in this case, it does more. The music helps to
bridge the gap between familiar entertainment devices and the
slice of reality portrayed, making them one and the same. It also*

helps those listening to forget that their diversion derives from spying on spectacles of pain, suffering, social and psychological dysfunction, and family disintegration. The audience is reassured that they are not voyeurs eavesdropping on what ought to be private conversations . . . not really. After all, it's just a show that they're watching, and they're taking the subject as seriously as the music tells them to take it, just the way it works in a sad movie.

JuJu, fifteen, has tattoos running up most of the surface of her arms and legs. She cries a lot during the brief time she's allotted to be a media attraction. So does her mother, who is occasionally photographed sitting backstage with two other mothers in the same predicament. All three have the eyes of frightened deer paralyzed by the headlights of an approaching death engine.

By contrast, the host's eyes on camera look self-confident but concerned. From time to time, he joins his guests on stage and speaks in low tones, as if no one else is listening to him elicit information from these troubled girls and to dispense soothing dollops of "advice." Before one commercial break, he tells the audience that these young women and their mothers have been brought here to be helped, not to air their dirty laundry; before another, he issues a similar disclaimer, promising to "give them things," to offer help and follow up, to track them as they put their lives back together as a result of this appearance. "Aftercare," some call it. He wants the girls—and, ultimately, the world—to see just how serious he's taking all of these proceedings, and the performance is fairly convincing, except when the camera's eye catches him looking away, probably getting his cues from the director.

Through her crying, JuJu says that she sincerely wants to put her life in order, and it's easy enough to believe that. But when Montel asks the high-school dropout what she wants to do, JuJu replies that she wants to be a "pioneer brain surgeon." He doesn't ask what she means by that curious phrase. He doesn't ask how she expects to achieve this goal realistically, given her academic record, her family circumstances, and her lack of financial resources. He simply nods his head in supportive understanding. The statement takes its place on the stage with the other props in this theater of the absurd.

The best drama is saved for last. First, Montel brings out Dr. Joy Browne, who's identified as a radio psychologist with a program that is syndicated to over 200 stations, and then JuJu's teary-eyed mother, Julie. After Montel admonishes JuJu repeatedly to "look at your mom," as if the girl hasn't seen her mother's desperation before, the psychologist can begin her healing work. "When you give advice," she asks Julie, "does the word 'sermon' come to mind?" "You're the mom." "We don't hit, no matter what. Can you promise you won't hit JuJu?" His hired healer having "saved" mother and daughter with these therapeutic words, Montel has a surprise. He brings out JuJu's sister, Chrissie, whom she hasn't seen in six months. Now there are three women crying and hugging on stage.

The camera comes in for a tight shot before the commercial break, after which we will hear from Brandi, an obese thirteen-year-old who looks far older than her years. A red bow is tied in her hair, making a mockery of the childhood Brandi has probably been denied. But there's hope . . . always hope. The promised subject flashes on the screen before the break: "Coming Up—Overweight Girl Makes Peace with Mom." Everything is going to be all right. (August 1995)

In our information age it's especially true that the messages we receive from the various media we are exposed to require constant questioning. If we passively sit back and receive unexamined messages, failing or refusing to consider not only *what* is said to us but *how* and *why*, we are open to the grossest kinds of manipulation, passing itself off as "entertainment." In that case, Jefferson's "wholesome discretion" becomes impossible.

Perhaps more than any other brand of media message that we receive, television talk programs deliberately use such gross manipulation in their attempt to entertain and supposedly "inform" us. While they employ a deceptive, game-like atmosphere, the information they provide about "real life," claiming that it's just a "reflection" of reality, is worse than useless. It's dangerous to play with and at deviance, for it puts us in the habit of "entertaining sin" in both senses of that phrase—using the moral errors and deviance of others for our entertainment and tolerating such behavior as a normal part of life. As we've noted, games are supposed to be played for fun, but this one isn't so much fun when it threatens to spill over into the nonplaying world. Here we look at the nature of the deceptive pseudogame, the techniques that are used to blur the distinction between play and the everyday world. (Later, we will consider the behind-the-scenes players and the business interests that make the game possible and profitable.)

The Players

Like all sporting contests and board games, the pseudogame of talk TV first requires players, willing participants who agree to leave the real world for a while and to enter the play world, abiding by its contrived laws, suspending belief in the rules of life as we know it, climbing into the game frame. This particular game has three main players: the host, the guests, and the studio audience. Of course, beyond the last of these, there is the television-viewing audience, but this group, although numerically vast, is passive in terms of the actual play, something like the television viewer of professional sports. As we shall see, however, the home audience is really not passive at all in the last analysis since it is they who will carry the value projections of the game into the real world, thus breaking the play frame.

As in all entertainment programs, we begin with the star of the show, and, in our time, star quality is critically important to the success of any theatrical enterprise. Movies, theater, concerts, recordings, and television programs that feature stars draw crowds, and the bigger the star, the bigger the box office. To be sure, talk-show stars are big box office for the little box. Geraldo and Donahue and Oprah are recognizable "one-name" celebrities, who like their counterparts in sports and show business, are photographed wherever they go, are hounded for autographs, and are venerated by our culture, whose fascination with celebrity is seemingly endless.

Like other theatrical actors talk-show stars are performers, and in this capacity they have assumed in their work roles personas that differ from their real-life selves. We know nothing about stage and screen actors or singers just by watching their staged work except that they can carry the role off. But a big difference exists between the talk-show celebrity and the theatrical star. While we fully expect actors to step out of their roles once they are off the stage, we have no such expectation for the talk-show performer.[1] (We tend to regard newscasters in the same way, incidentally.) We expect that what we see on "stage" in terms of care, concern, intelligence, and sensitivity is what we get off the little screen as well, and if the star player can make us believe just that, then he or she is playing the role well.

The specific role that these individuals are called upon to play is that of *host*. That term has a very specific meaning and very clear connotation in our culture. A host is a person who receives and entertains guests in a familiar, nonthreatening setting, often his or her home. The host is responsible for seeing to it that the guests are made comfortable and that they are at ease interacting with other invited guests. On the surface, the talk-show host operates in much the same way. He or she represents a reassuring familiar face welcoming into a familiar place guests who think they "know" the host. (In fact, if the hosts changed every day, it would not work at all.) Everyone present is on a first-name basis, everyone is made comfortable at the start of play: we're all friends here, we're all in this together.

Acting in the role of enabler, the host is there to put the guest and audience at their ease and to facilitate easy discussion—regardless of how bizarre, heinous, or cruel the topic or the player's behavior may be—thus providing a stable basis for the game. Accordingly, unlike the guest, who will be changed by this game, the host's real life is not unduly affected by the nature of the talk; all is of a piece, and the show goes on day after day. Whether the guest is an unwed mother trying to pull her life together or a serial rapist claiming to be a victim of society, the host always begins the game in the very same way—politely welcoming guests, making sure they feel comfortable and prepared to speak about their "problems," often expressing, at least in the hosts' welcoming remarks, nonjudgmental concern and objectivity, ensuring what will take place during the next hour (minus commercials) is just some friendly, societally useful conversation among equals. If the guest is a teenaged drug addict wearing torn clothing and living on the street and the host is a man wearing a $1,200 suit and living on Fifth Avenue, no matter. The host's role is to make them look all the same.

The guests, on the other hand, seem to have an easier role than the host's. Whereas the host has a number of professional tasks to carry out in order to keep the game going, guests principally have one role—to talk provocatively, to confess, to express their feelings. As the center of attention (and often of controversy), guests must stick to the prescribed subject, whether or not it fully represents the contexts in which they live their lives. Let's say that the guest is a dentist with a predilection for child molesting. He must speak only of that topic, not about his practice of dentistry or his golf score. Although not a professional actor like the host, the guest, too, must fit into a role that may have comparatively little to do with his real life, and the audience (in this case, both the studio and home viewers) must believe that they "know" him just as they "know" the host. By contrast, the audience, who are really no different from the guests in real life, are made to believe that they are somehow different from and superior to the guest in this game, owing primarily to the fact that the guests have something to confess and the audience has the right to hear, judge, and counsel.

The studio audience's role is the easiest of the three. Like the ancient Greek chorus they comment on the action. They function much like the fans at a ball game or the spectators at the crap tables in Atlantic City or, unfortunately, like participants in a new-age therapy group. Initially brought together to see their favorite television star, the host, they are free to sit there, observe, and possibly participate in the interrogation of the guests. Of these audience "roles," however, this last "role" is the most disturbing and potentially socially problematic one. Let's bear in mind that they are usually a crowd of people who have stood in line to see a show, knowing neither the subject of the program nor the guests in advance. After only a few minutes of listening to the guests' stories, the audience is coached and encouraged to feel free enough to give advice on intimate subjects to people who will enter and leave their lives in a matter of an hour at best. The complicated social and personal lives of people are distilled and commented upon by total strangers in the course of a brief meeting.

Needless to say, the whole thing is patently ridiculous. Even old-time gossips usually confined their talk to those in their own communities, people they had some personal knowledge of, and contact with, in everyday life. In real life, moreover, the "confessant" and the listener would probably never meet in public and begin this kind of interaction. Why, then, do we accept it when we see it on TV? Or, turning that question around, if the TV version of reality is "valid" and everyone is an "open book" to be read in a four-minute encounter, why bother to spend the time and energy it takes to get to know people? In fact, taking our cues from television, many people might think that such social "interaction" is transferable to real life, and that's a worrisome thought indeed.

The studio audience's main role, though, is cheering and jeering, adding emotional intensity and an air of authenticity and immediacy to the proceedings. Without their presence, the dynamic of the game would be vastly different, resembling more a tabloid-television show (e.g., *A Current Affair*, *Inside Edition*) than a "useful" and "practical" discussion of everyday American life. Imagine a sporting event played in silence, without a crowd of reactive fans. That's what the talk-show game would look like without the studio players.

Apart from their role as cheering/jeering fans, moreover, they are there for a variety of other purposes, and while admission to the game may be free, there are expectations imposed on them, too. Individually, they come forward to ask questions, share anecdotes, offer therapeutic advice, express opinions, challenge interpretations, even physically confront at times. Collectively, they must react "appropriately" to the juicy revelations and heartfelt confessions. Their reactions are expected to be visible and often audible. Apart from the host, whose celebrity status brings the home viewers in, the studio audience is most crucial for connecting the program content to the millions of television viewers out there. Indeed, the guests themselves do not seem to differ from the studio audience, which further solidifies the connection. Home viewers are comforted by, and identify with, the presence and reactions of these "everyday" people, thus bringing the people from the TV audience into the game, regardless of their physical distance from the playing field.

The Rules of Play

All games have rules, and these rules must be understood by all players. Formal game rules are typically codified and, in professional games, invariable. (In informal games among friends, rules are sometimes altered on the spot by agreement, but hardly ever are they changed enough to create an entirely new game.) At times prospective players learn these rules simply by reading them on a game box or in a manual, but more often they learn them through observation and instruction by the initiated. In that way, a common game experience is transmitted to all players, and the games can be perpetuated by imitation.

The rules of the talk-television game are not codified in quite the same way as are the game rules that come with Monopoly. Rather, they are transmitted by observation, imitation, and coaching by the program producers. The fact that these shows are highly produced (to "manage shocks," among other things) is often overlooked. The salaried producers are largely responsible for choosing topics, getting and screening guests, making guests comfortable enough to open up, and scripting the proceedings, which participants can often read right off the rolling TelePrompTers. These behind-the-scenes people are, in effect, the "brains" of the shows. (Later we will discuss the larger "brains" behind the scenes, the equity of the owners/producers and syndicators.) Interestingly, many of the personnel on the talk shows move to competitors' programs, a fact that may explain in part the similarities among all of the shows in this genre. Unlike the major corporate players, these lesser sharks also tend to view themselves as "politically correct liberals," people who privately disavow the shows and argue that, if they didn't produce them, others would. "I only work here" is the general refrain that allows them to displace responsibility back to the audiences who supposedly want this stuff, the prospective participants who write or call their ideas in, and the free market system in general. One industry insider, Lora Wiley, who has worked for both Jerry Springer and Geraldo Rivera, has said, "Some people contend that we contribute to the degeneration of society. . . . But I maintain we're not the cause of it, we're the result" (Stasio 253). Our point is, however, that they do *contribute* to society's degeneration regardless of the original "cause" of this social breakdown. A drug dealer can't excuse his activity by claiming not to have been the inventor of the drugs or the cause of the abuser's addiction. Such arguments all turn out to be very self-righteous and deliberately confusing.

As for the rules of the game they play, there are ten common ones although there are some small variations among the talk shows:

1. The guest must talk provocatively about the prescribed subject to the exclusion of all other "irrelevant" aspects of his or her life.

2. The guest must confess all and is not encouraged to remain silent, assert that a topic is none of the host's and studio audience's business, or leave the stage.

3. The guest must appear to be an understandable and representative American regardless of appearance and the nature of confession. At the same time, however, the guest's actions, words, and/or appearance must be bizarre enough to be entertaining and to allow the audience to feel "smug" about not being like him or her.

4. The guest need not be informed in advance of surprise guests, unexpected personal information to be disclosed publicly about him or her, forced "outings," and other revelations.

5. The host must welcome and continuously interact with the guest in a familiar manner, often using his or her first name, regardless of the nature of the subject for discussion or the character of the guest.

6. The host must appear at all times interested, knowledgeable, concerned, sensitive and "appropriately upset," carrying the game forward regardless of how silly or scandalous the revelations may be.

7. The host cannot reveal the true nature (goal) of the game by telling guests that they are interesting or boring, important or insignificant, only in terms of the show's ratings for the day.

8. Neither the host nor the guest must regard any subject as taboo or inappropriate for public discourse. The object of disclosure is to let the guest speak without immediate dismissal.

9. The studio audience must act as participants by reacting visibly and audibly to the guest's revelations in response to the host's interrogation of the guest.

10. All players—the host, the studio audience, and other guests—are encouraged to provide advice, counsel, observations, therapy, praise, and censure of the guest under consideration.

Winning Strategies

So much for the rules, but how is the game won? As is the case with all games, winning this particular sport requires strategy and cunning. Let's say a National League baseball team is narrowly losing a game, and they manage to load the bases in the seventh inning with two outs and the pitcher batting next. Although the National League's official rules of play do not allow for a designated hitter, neither do they prevent the manager from suddenly deciding on a pitching change so that he can use a pinch hitter in this crucial situation. So it is with all games. While some spell out strategies for success, most do not codify such information. Rather, the successful players are the ones who devise ways to manipulate the rules in order to win. The television-talk game has its own winning strategies, but since we are dealing here not with sporting competition but the "magical" and primarily fictional world of television art, we prefer to see strategies as the illusions created to promote and sustain interest.

Life Imitates Art

The first illusion concerns the milieu—the mood, setting, assumptions, and point of view—created through the technical manipulation of the medium. These involve things like the careful and artistic use of selective editing, graphics, camera angles, and music. Before looking at the way in which talk shows play with these techniques, however, let's consider some of the assumptions we make when we consume art.

It is true that, at some level, all art imitates life, but it is also true that this particular brand of imitation takes a very distinct form within a context which we are calling a "frame." Art is actually a controlled conspiracy between imagination and real life. In their imaginative construction of fictional stories, writers typically select their materials from everyday reality and arrange them in an orderly fashion so that they make artistic sense to readers, who agree to enter the frame world of the fiction. These readers know that, unlike real life—which is alternatively spontaneous and routine, messy and orderly, predictable and exciting, boring and interesting—the successful narrative world is always tightly controlled, fascinating, and orderly. It has a clear beginning, middle, and end. Moreover, simple solutions to complex problems are not hard to bring about in art because the magician behind the machine controls all things. Solutions in life, of course, are another matter altogether, but we can easily understand and accept the differences between our lives and our fictions because the frames are different. As a sage person once noted, "[T]he very notion of resolution is a sentimental deception."

A specific kind of narrative art—indeed, before television, the kind from which most people in our society received their fictions—is film. While the narrative frame is comparable to the one we find in prose fiction, the medium itself is different because of the manner in which the story is told. Added to the idea of artistic selection and imposition of order are the audio-visual techniques used to tell the story, and again, by knowing the frame, we know the rules of the game and can distinguish it from everyday life. In real-life situations, for instance, we expect stimuli to come at us from all directions, and even solemn moments can be broken by uncontrolled and spontaneous stimuli—say, a person sneezing loudly during a funeral eulogy. On the other hand, although film narratives create illusions of life, true spontaneity is not permissible. Dramatic twists and turns that appear shockingly spontaneous are actually scripted, and true spontaneous events like a ladder falling onto the set are edited out. Moreover, it is not your eye that finds what is interesting to look at from among the available stimuli, but the camera's eye. Careful editing of the images in that eye then ensures viewer fascination. To heighten dramatic effect even more and to efficiently establish mood, appropriate music accompanies the edited image we finally see. Sad music doesn't usually play during life's heartbreaking events, but it usually does during a heartbreaking scene in a movie. That's just the way things work, and we accept all of them as long as we understand the fictional vs. the real frames in which they (and we) are meant to operate.

Television uses comparable techniques, and we accept them there, too. But television—by far the most pervasive and invasive medium in our daily lives—goes much farther, for it often employs the materials of fiction in its presentation of real-life situations (mixing frames). News programs represent a prime example. Like dramatic fiction, all of them begin and end with "appropriate" theme music. All of them also present the news using a narrative (often dramatic) structure—selecting, arranging, and editing details—much as fiction writers do to create credible, coherent stories. Finally, all of them use the camera's eye to focus our attention. The television coverage of the O. J. Simpson trial was a good case in point. Ponderous, almost Wagnerian theme music was used to set a tone of gravity for this real-life drama. The camera continually focused on "interesting" scenes. If the coroner provided a graphic interpretation of the brutal murders of Nicole Simpson and Ronald Goldman, the camera found O. J.'s face, looking for a reactive shot. Although real trials (this one included) have a large number of boring moments in which legal procedural business is conducted, news programs give us only the juicy stuff from this slice of life—precisely what a fiction writer does. The confusion of messy, boring life and neat riveting drama is inevitable. And since most Americans get their news today from television rather than newspapers, it can be downright dangerous, especially in light of the fact that we are going about the business of our own real lives as we consume these images.[2] Whereas the darkened theater and the printed page represent frames in themselves, the images on the TV playing in the family room are a part of the everyday life going on around them.

Talk television, which is also supposed to be concerned with real life, uses the same techniques and because it's dealing with everyday people talking about private matters in a game format, it's more disconcerting. The deceptive techniques for winning the "game" (in this case, the ratings game) also begin with theme music—familiar sounds that are employed at the beginning, before commercial breaks, and the end, providing a stable and familiar base from which to proceed. The music is sometimes slowed or accelerated in the course of the program in accordance with the topic generally and the dramatic moments of the program specifically.

The camera is also used to provide riveting drama. Unlike the human eye which follows random stimuli, the camera's eye is strictly trained on the stars-for-a-day, the guests, alternating between long shots of the panel on stage and close-ups of the individual confessants. Close-up shots of the real star, the host, are also frequent, and this technique showcases the host's performance skills as he or she shows appropriately registered objectivity, concern, outrage, disbelief, sympathetic support, and so on. The studio audience also appears on camera periodically, but they are, as a group, more problematical and unpredictable than the other "stars." They are, after all, just people who have stood in line to see a theatrical exhibition starring their favorite daytime personality. Although the producers promise to provide the illusion of unscripted real-life drama, they are not about to tell the studio audience that the program is highly controlled, with guests often given instructions on what to say, how explicitly to say it, even what to wear. Nevertheless, there are some unpredictable theatrical lapses. The audience members may appear restless or self-conscious or adjust their clothing or look at their watches or get up and head for the bathroom. In that case, random shots would break the fictional frame, and so the producers must take only reactive shots of the audience as they register shock, amusement, anger, and other emotions.

Finally, of course, the whole is carefully edited to get rid of the boring stuff, to fit the material within the program's time limits, and to achieve maximum (even threatening) dramatic tension. In much the same way that hundreds of hours of theatrical film are edited into a tight ninety-minute movie, so several hours of videotape become forty-five minutes of television entertainment. Even the commercials, which ought to break the dramatic mood (imagine a movie with commercials between scenes), are brilliantly integrated, used for a timeout or a break from the story and bringing another kind of contrived "real life" into our homes along with the images seen on the talk shows. The realistic frame, in short, is deceptive, and this particular fiction is passed off as a slice of real life—life as art.

Just the "Facts"

To say the least, the human mind is complex, and even people who are troubled in one particular area can live relatively normal lives in every other respect. To recycle the example we used earlier, a man may have a predilection for child abuse and still be an excellent dentist, a golfer with an enviable handicap, a loving husband and father, and a contributing member of society. This particular man would probably not look, act, or smell like a monster—not in real life anyway.

However, that sort of rounded projection of human life won't pass muster in the ratings game, and the winning strategy here involves focusing the entire portrayal of this person on his desire to receive and inflict pain. If that means ignoring the entire context in which his life is lived, then so be it. This is, after all, a game, and games have every right to be selective in their enactments of reality. Here are several highly effective techniques:

- Captions or subtitles known as chyrons are used to "define" the guest. If the chyron beneath the close-up shot of the dentist says "child abuser," then that is what he *is*, why he's there, and all other information about him becomes either irrelevant or interesting only in the context of his confession. If a show is about "out-of-control teenagers," the weight of an obese mother sitting there would not be an issue, whereas her weight would be highlighted if the show were about "obese mothers." In other words, the chyron tells one what to focus on.

- Each show is focused on a particular theme, and the guests are treated as variations on that theme rather than as individuals with unique biographies.

- Although the full biographical context of the guest's life is basically extraneous material, the audience must be made to feel as if they "know" the guest. This knowledge is basically the result of what little we are told about him and/or what he himself confesses. The credibility of his story, particularly in light of the limited time in which it is told, must not be questioned too closely, and if it is, the guest's truthfulness is to be measured by how sympathetic he appears and how forthcoming he has been with confession.

- Dramatic turns are most effective in focusing the game. Surprise guests hidden from the participants' view, outings, shocking public revelations, and other such devices ensure dramatic tension and corroboration of the singular program theme.

Flattening the Round

For better or worse, we carry all of our cultural biases into our encounters with people, especially brief encounters. If an attractive woman in a business suit were to approach you in a crowded place during daylight hours to ask directions, you'd be more likely to stop and help than you would if any of the delimiters mentioned were altered—appearance, setting, time of day, perhaps even gender. (Not incidentally, successful con artists know how to exploit all of these biases.) By contrast, when we know a person well, all of these variables become far less important, even completely insignificant.

In literary analysis, characters are sometimes studied using the concepts of "roundness" and "flatness." Round (or dynamic) characters are multifaceted, presented as three-dimensional people with strengths and flaws; flat (or static) characters, on the other hand, are those whom the author leaves one-dimensional, showing us only a particular side of his or her personality. If we apply this way of looking at characters to television talk shows, we find something very interesting—and very deceptive—taking place. Because of the genre's time and deliberate thematic limitations, guests (the characters of this particular fiction) are flattened and one-dimensional, like comic-book characters complete with talking balloons over their heads. However, at the same time, the audience is given the illusion that they "know" these people and are therefore in a position to judge and advise them. (Actually, by the time they come forward with advice, audience members have only heard from these strangers for about three minutes.) Likewise, the audience also has the illusion that they "know" the real star of the show, the host, even better since he or she is a familiar "friend" who appears on television every day and acts the same during each friendly encounter: concerned, helpful, knowing, wise, objective, sensitive, and unflappable. In reality, though, the host is a character in a real-life fiction, and for all of his or her seeming familiarity, this individual is even more "flat" than the guest since the persona that he or she reveals to us is more tightly scripted than that of the guest.

The effective creation of this illusion of familiarity is crucial to the success of the talk game. The audience's implied trust in the host and snap judgments of the contestants must occur efficiently if the game is to work, and to carry this process off, these programs must use our cultural biases, our "blueprints," against us. How is it done?

First and foremost, those guests who are the most likable and sympathetic are considered to be the most truthful. In fact, regardless of how odious the confession is, guests will be congratulated for their honesty and bravery if they maintain a pleasant and polite persona. By contrast, those who are contemptuous of the audience and/or of society at large are rejected, even if their judgments are valid. Such guests are typically chided for telling tales or gossiping irresponsibly or violating confidences.

Regardless of how flagrant the guests' confessions are, moreover, the host is always asking the audience to let them tell their side of the story (as if all admissions were formal arguments) and saying to the guests things like "We need to hear what you have to say" and "My audience wants to know your story." An illusion is thus created that the host is really a friend when in actuality he or she is only enabling the guests to strip themselves for public amusement. The overall effect is to make the host look reasonable to the audience and the confessant often more bizarre in his tastes, opinions, attitudes, and the like. Despite this, however, the ongoing discussion manages to give the illusion that these guests are representative members of society rather than an extremely biased and self-selected sampling of people desperate enough for attention or unstable enough to allow themselves to be made public spectacles. They feel cared about and thus drop whatever social guards they possess against public humiliation and stigma. This game is analogous to the gambling practice of "comping" losers in order to make them feel important and appreciated. In this way, television becomes a "safe place," giving them a sense that they are somehow beyond the bounds of normal public consequences.

Although, at least at the beginning of play, the host is supposedly objective and protective toward the guests, "on their side," they are often left to tell their stories alone onstage, unprotected, while the host wanders among the audience. This is more often the case on the newer and more successful programs (Jerry Springer, Ricki Lake, Jenny Jones), than on the earlier shows, in which Oprah Winfrey and Phil Donohue would usually sit on stage with their guests. The effect of leaving them alone is to isolate them while the host, however objective he or she may claim to be, is physically and intellectually *with* the audience, thereby increasing, without any real cause, his or her own credibility with them. Hosts tend to return to sit or stand near guests who are in danger of "breaking frame" or leaving the "game" (stage). They may even try to comfort them by physically holding them, touching them, or offering them a tissue. If all of this fails, they go to station break, and after the break, the guest has usually been cajoled into returning. Few leave for the duration of the broadcast. Eventually, some hosts (especially Geraldo and Montel) actually turn on the guests, attacking them personally for their disclosures, without which, ironically, the program would fail.

In turn, the audience, many of whom we've implied resemble the guests in condition, educational level, and some other factors, attack the guests too, for the audience members are given the illusion that they are somehow different from, better than, those telling their tales. All audience members appear equally credible in this populist, egalitarian, democratic world, and because of that illusion, they can feel good about what would normally be considered despicable behavior—eavesdropping on private matters, giggling at titillating disclosures, egging on the guests to provide more lurid detail. In general, the message is that the entire microcosm of the talk show (guests, hosts, producers, audience members in the studio and at home, advertisers) and the societal macrocosm are *all in this together*. In fact, the main problem is that, at some level, we are!

The seeming "normality" of these proceedings is important for maintaining conversation. If the confession were to appear beyond the pale of normal, useful talk, people would reject as outlandish what they were hearing. To the contrary, such talk often leads to requests for even more graphic description, which is gladly provided. The illusion created is that this talk is socially necessary and practical and that it can take place anywhere at any time and with anyone without social repercussion. Imagine being in a supermarket when a stranger comes up and says, "I think it's important that you know that my wife just ran off with my best friend." At that point, you'd probably run, too. But watching the talk-show game is different. Nothing is outrageous, including surprise guests with information about the contestant and public outings. Few revelations, however shocking, are met with "that's none of our business." No one is supposed to say, "How dare you ask such an inappropriate question?" as one likely would in real life. No one feels threatened enough to run for the hills or call the cops. Less drastically but no less effective, one rarely walks out of the studio or even turns the television set off. But we have evidence to suggest that people do consider these confessions outrageous in real life. When many guests return home, they find that they are indeed shunned and hated by their *real* friends and neighbors, looked upon as embarrassing pariahs.

Therapy in the Arena

Therapy, like surgery, is not a spectator sport carried out for our entertainment. And yet, one of the chief strategies of the talk shows is to present the illusion that since confession is supposedly good for both the individual and collective social souls, the advice offered to troubled confessants by hosts, audience members, call-in viewers, and pop psychologists can help to heal both the guest and the greater society whose "problem" he or she supposedly represents. None of us is privy to the training (or lack thereof), theories, track records, or biases of these particular "therapists." Legitimate therapists, needless to say, do not practice in televised soundbites, and talk-show performers and their audiences are not in a position to "heal" anyone. In *Tuning in Trouble*, the authors, Jeanne Heaton and Nona Wilson, who interviewed Abt, agree that "the shows make a mockery of the mental health profession" and indicate their own concern when therapy is reduced to "the level of sound-bite sensation" (5).

Of course, the purpose of the confessants' disclosures is entertainment, not therapy, and that entertainment has been known to go to bizarre lengths. For a while Oprah and others were devoting shows to hair-raising stories by "adult children" who suddenly remembered repressed memories of childhood incest and other parental abuses. These people would appear to tell their shocking tales on television, often with their own or the resident "therapist" and sometimes their horrified aging parents trying to defend themselves. Because many of these parents have brought legal actions against such therapists for "brainwashing" troubled people into believing they remembered things that never actually happened, there are virtually no shows devoted to this topic any longer. So much for the social usefulness of these therapeutic programs. This is not to say that all repressed memories are false, only that they are not easily validated phenomena and, more important, that talk shows are not able to deal with the complexities of human memory, disturbed familial relationships, and complicated interactions and emotions.

Rather, they treat all subjects briefly (between frequent commercial breaks) and in black and white terms with easy answers and quick fixes. This approach, which is more appropriate for entertainment than for healing, is responsible for generating a variety of socially dangerous illusions:

- That quick fixes to complex problems are possible in a public airing, working out with a few minutes of "advice" the difficulties of a lifetime, as if coming clean were enough

- That appearing on the show is "therapy" in itself and, if really necessary, that people will follow up the quick-fix therapy with more traditional long-term therapy, though the hosts and producers rarely provide systematic evidence of such follow-up or its efficacy

- That all therapy is equally useful or, indeed, that it works at all most of the time (criminologists today pretty much agree that verbal therapy for sex offenders, for instance, doesn't usually work)

- That the personal revelations of troubled people will help to heal comparable problems within society itself (e.g., teenage pregnancy), since their problems, insights, and solutions are assumed to be universal

- That pop "psychobabble" or trite homilies or generalized panaceas (e.g., developing self-esteem) will repair the failures brought about by illness, economic deprivation, educational inadequacy, and other cultural conditions

- That audience members, hosts, and "legitimate" therapists are in a position to give therapeutic advice or reject as "freaks" those beyond the help of two-minute healing sessions

- That large social forces—economic, political, historical, bureaucratic—are subordinate to pop concepts like "hugging your inner child," "getting in touch with your higher power,"

"self-esteem," "communication," and getting away from "co-
dependency" and "enabling"

- That emotional moments like forgiving reunions, replete with
  close-up shots of crying participants who are "sorry" for their
  past actions, are anything more than the stuff of fiction
  applied to real-world problems

- That people who have engaged in or have been victims of
  such serious offenses as incest or rape can be rapidly rehabili-
  tated, or at the very least helped by confession, advice, or
  "finding God" and that there need be no irrevocable consequences (emotional pain, stigma) of these actions.

Knowing how a magician manages to perform a sleight-of-hand
illusion may wreck the entertainment value of the trick, but the
sleight-of-hand illusions performed by talk shows, although seemingly mere entertainment, may be contributing to the wrecking of
our common civil culture. Only by understanding the game, the
players, and strategies does the viewer—and the culture—have a
better chance to win.

At this point, it is appropriate to consider some tentative
answers to the difficult question, why now? In chapter 5, we look
at the confluence of social, political, and cultural factors that set
the stage for toxic talk.

Notes

1. Montel Williams's nonexploitative persona may have been
undermined by June 1996 stories that some female employees have
accused him of sexual harassment and that he reportedly held production
staff meetings while he was dressed in his underwear (Speers F2).

2. This troubling blurring of news and entertainment has been
widely discussed. See especially Ken Auletta, *Three Blind Mice: How
the TV Networks Lost Their Way* (New York: Random House, 1991); and
Neil Postman and Steve Powers, *How to Watch TV News* (New York:
Penguin, 1992).

5

The Social Vacuum

The multitude has suddenly become visible. . . . Before, if it existed, it passed unnoticed, occupying the background of the social stage; now it has advanced to the footlights and is the principal character. There are no longer protagonists; there is only the chorus.

—Jose Ortega y Gasset,
The Revolt of the Masses (1932)

The "Victorian era"—the height of print culture—was a time of "secrets." People were fascinated with the multiple layers and depths of life. . . . Our own age, in contrast, is fascinated by exposure. Indeed, the act of exposure itself now seems to excite us more than the content of the secrets exposed. The steady stripping away of layers of social behavior has made the "scandal" and the revelation of the "deep dark secret" every-day occurrences. Ironically, what is pulled out of the closets that contain seemingly extraordinary events is, ultimately, the "ordinariness" of everyone. The unusual becomes the usual."

—Joshua Meyrowitz,
No Sense of Place (1985)

One trend that bothers me is the glorification of stupidity, that the media are reassuring people that it's all right not to know anything. That to me is far more dangerous than a little pornography on the Internet. Teens should be surrounded by people who know deep things.

—Carl Sagan,
Seattle's Pacific Rim
Trans-Tech Conference, 2 August 1995

Ricki Lake: Even the title of the program is in your face: "Today I'm Gonna Tell You Why I Dumped You." It's about five couples of ex-lovers, one of each finding out why they're now "ex"—right there on network TV.

There's Polly and Sam. Polly says Sam goes out in his Corvette with his friends and tries to pick up her female friends. She admits, though, that she's lied to him in the past. She said that she was 23 years old, but admits here that she's really only 19.

There's Sidney and Latisha. They don't agree on very much. He claims that they went out together for four years; she says it was only two. Latisha argues that Sidney cared for her too much and that she didn't want to hurt him. Her way of letting him down easily was to wait until he showed up at her house one day and slam the door in Sidney's face. Sidney denies that he'd had a door slammed on him. He claims that she asked some friends to tell him that they were through.

There's Jackie and Ronald. While he's confessing, she sits backstage with headphones on, listening in. The camera's eye alternates between his testimony, her backstage eavesdropping, and obligatory audience-reaction shots. And there is a lot to react to here. The reason he dumped her, he says, is that he suddenly discovered he was gay. While he was dating her, he met a young man he also went out with. At first, there was nothing sexual about their encounters, just going out. After a while, though, they fell in love. Jackie is brought out then, and Rikki asks the only question to ask in this situation: how does Jackie feel about what she's just heard? Ricki must have been disappointed. Jackie doesn't have much to say at all; she doesn't even look that bothered by the whole thing. And when Ron says that he cares for her as a friend and wants to go on with her in that capacity, she says the feeling's mutual and agrees.

There's Matt and Sarah. At first, Matt says that she moved to Ohio and began flirting with other men. Then he claims that that was not the reason for leaving her. It was much worse—she was abusive, he maintains, and has even tried to kill him, once by pushing him down the stairs and by throwing a big knife at him another time. Sarah goes on the defensive. He was living with another girl, she accuses, and besides, she didn't really throw the big knife at him, only near where he was standing. Her little brother was there when it happened, and he could vouch for her!

There's Tyrone and Evelyn. Tyrone says that she was cheating on him, and he's got proof: she was pregnant once. She says that baby was his; he says it wasn't. Then Evelyn shifts the ground, saying that they weren't really steady lovers anyway. They were just friends who slept together once. Again, Tyrone denies what she's saying, but she insists it's true. Besides, she already had a steady boyfriend when they slept together!

There's more. . . . "Dr. Judy," Ricki's sometime resident therapist, is there to dispense her sound-bite advice to the couples. Then, the doorbell rings on stage, and in comes Ru Paul, a male transvestite musician. He/she struts around on stage to music and gags with the players, joking at one point that he/she was once Ron's roommate. The program concludes with Ru Paul distributing free copies of his/her autobiography—to Ricki, to Dr. Judy, to the guests, and to every single person in the studio audience. Confession, therapy, promotion, and uproarious entertainment, all in a single hour! (July 1995)

The idea of our being spectators to enactments of life is hardly new. At least since the rise of drama in fifth-century Athens, people have been fascinated by the "game" of eavesdropping on the lives of others, becoming, so to speak, the "fourth wall" in a private room. By the time Greece's imperial successor, Rome, took over this form of entertainment two centuries later, the spectators had become jaded enough to require more for their money. Like contemporary America, Rome's was a technical civilization, where material artifacts flourished, not the symbolic products of verbal art. High moral comedy gave way to farce, and the decorously presented, off-stage violence of Greek tragedy was replaced by the sensationally popular Senecan revenge plays, which were filled with plenty of stage blood and guts. Eventually this taste for blood as entertainment evolved out of the theatrical frame to include the gladiatorial displays and public executions that took place in the Colosseum.[1] So what if real people died in these theatrical diversions? People *wanted* these entertainments. Perhaps they also served the political interests of the state to encourage such "entertainment" as they functioned to distract the citizenry from the real political and economic problems of the day. By the same token, however, it can be argued that these self-same "distractions" contributed to "the decline and fall" of classic civilizations.

Something analogous to the degeneration in form, taste, and standards of public conduct described above happened in America's television age, only, owing to the high-tech nature of that medium, the evolutionary period was sharply compressed—from about two centuries to about two decades. In a 1996 piece on incivility in our society, James Morris puts the matter well: "Pop culture could not be so invasive without technology to lend it a saturation power" (30). Indeed, television has managed to invade the American home—and psyche—within a relatively brief span of time. The mass transmission of television images and the mass production of television sets occurred in the late 1940s, and these factors radically and forever changed the way people receive information and are entertained. The neat frames that separated reality from artifact in all of the other modern media—print, radio, and film—began to erode virtually from the outset, as did the taste of its consumers. Even the spectacles put on at the Roman Colosseum, incidentally, had framing mechanisms, namely the special and occasional nature of the performances and the need to join a social group to participate.[2] The new medium, with its exciting images and its ease of consumption, required neither special skills nor the inconvenience of leaving home and gathering with others. It was an instant success, and although it didn't drive the other media out of business entirely, it did affect their content, and it certainly put an enormous dent in their popularity and consumption.[3]

Still, for the first decade and a half of television, customary separate frames of a sort were maintained by the early network producers and accepted by the viewing public. News programs were meant to inform; comedies, dramas, and variety shows were meant to entertain; and the two were clearly separable in the minds of viewers. Walter Cronkite told us "the way it is," and Lassie and Lucy and Superman made us cry or laugh or be proud to be American, but they didn't cross over into one another's territory. Then, in November of 1963, shots rang out in Dealy Plaza in Dallas, cutting short the life of the thirty-fifth President of the United States, and the two territories began to merge.

Of course, it was not the President's assassination itself that brought about the change, but the manner in which the American people followed the sad developments.[4] Thanks to satellite feeds, the nation watched transfixed as all of the networks preempted regular programming for days and showed live transmissions followed by endless rerunnings of various scenes—the vigil at Parkland General Hospital, the grieving widow, the swearing-in of the new President, the arrival of the body in Washington, the funeral replete with the pathos of a riderless horse and two fatherless youngsters, the grave at Arlington, and so on. There were also repeatedly shown films of the shooting, retrospectives on the Kennedy family, soundbite interviews with "experts" and people on the street reacting to the national trauma. Even Walter Cronkite himself was choked up with emotion on live national television. Ted Turner's CNN was not the first to exploit the satellite feed, nor did it invent the idea that round-the-clock news coverage of sensational events could be entertaining. That idea was unleashed—in part spontaneously, in part owing to the coincidence of event and available technology—on November 22, 1963.

All of this coverage, brought to us in the name of news and national tragedy, meant ratings for the networks, but it also meant something else, something much more profound and lasting sociologically. It meant that we could feel like a community without having to be in a social situation, to participate, in Joshua Meyrowitz's words, in television's "shared arena." In his book *No Sense of Place: The Impact of Electronic Media on Social Behavior*, Meyrowitz argues that there was a kind of democratizing effect brought about by our viewing perceived reality on television: "Through television, rich and poor, young and old, scholars and illiterates, males and females, and people of all ages, professions, classes, and religions share the same or very similar information at the same moment. Through television, Americans may gain a strange sort of communion with each other. In times of crisis . . . millions of Americans sit in the glow of their television receivers and watch the same material over and over again in an effort, perhaps, to find comfort, see meaning, and feel united with all the other faceless viewers" (90).

This unity comes, it seems, at the expense of real social and civic interaction. Our collective hours of television watching, according to many educators and analysts, have also come at the expense of developing our intellectual abilities to grasp complex, abstract, ambiguous ideas and at the expense of the patience necessary to read difficult books, or even any books at all. At a time when our national illiteracy rates are higher than those of our major economic competitors in the global marketplace, surely the television-viewing public does itself no service to be watching mind-numbing, contradictory, and often incoherent talk about subjects either trivial in nature or made so in their presentation on talk television.[5] Our desire for a high standard of living, which must be based on the intellectual capital of a society today, is certainly undermined by the low standards of the daily, round-the-clock television talk shows.

Live, reality-based television made us dissatisfied with the traditional separation between information and entertainment or between fact and fiction. We now demand a new and more potent mix called "infotainment." Like the audiences in the Roman Colosseum long ago, we want to substitute real blood for the fake stage variety or, like the earlier Greeks, none at all, and commercial television obliges our taste so long as we watch and purchase their advertisers' products. Since the Kennedy assassination, the continuous live transmissions kept coming at us periodically—the murder of John F. Kennedy's alleged assassin, the assassinations of Bobby Kennedy and Martin Luther King, the walk on the moon, Watergate, the fall of Vietnam, the hostage situation in Iran, the assassination of John Lennon, the attempted assassinations of President Reagan and Pope John Paul II, NASA's Challenger disaster, ABSCAM, Iran-Contra, Operation Desert Storm (or, CNN's living-room war), and live coverage of assorted natural and contrived catastrophes, wars and conflicts, and scandals involving political leaders.

By now, after some thirty years of such infotainment, our taste for this heady brew can no longer be satisfied by periodic gulps, and so we have continuous showings of real life on CNN and, whenever possible (and profitable), the networks. All the world is indeed a stage, and its events have become theatrical diversions available on demand and right in our own homes. And these stage invasions are not limited to geographical space but also involve our civic institutions. Another Kennedy's rape trial direct from the courtroom held us spellbound recently, surpassed only by the low-speed chase, arrest, and murder trial of a football hero turned commercial endorser turned movie star. Sometimes reality is even staged, with real people performing for the camera, to heighten its dramatic appeal. Would the O. J. trial have been as "produced" for the media as it has been without their presence, particularly television? And this production was not limited to the trial itself. Talk shows of all types have been debating the implications of the trial for months and have featured "experts" (often real lawyers turned media personalities like CNN's Greta Van Sustern who, as a result of her daily commentaries on that trial, now has her own show, *Burden of Proof*) suggesting the need to change the procedural law. That the trial represented an anomaly and that over 90% of men, regardless of race, who are on trial for killing their spouses will be found guilty seems almost beside the point. We are expert daily consumers of entertaining reality now.

Talk television is happy to give us more supposed reality, and it has packaged the product in the appealing wrapper of socially useful entertainment. In that way, we could watch and listen to dysfunctional people tell their lurid tales, and we could be amused and diverted in much the same way as we are amused and diverted by the ongoing news coverage of important events. As many have already pointed out, we are a nation of consumers addicted to entertaining things, living for the moment, and television has become the center of our homes, our routines.[6] We regard its messages about life, whether presented in a straight news format or an entertaining talk show, as our most trusted sources of information about reality, and that is unfortunate. The air of authenticity in these talk shows is engrossing and, to some, as significant as, or even more compelling than, that of televised news, thus shaping perceptions about the world. We are, in Neil Postman's phrase, "amusing ourselves to death." This "death," of course, refers to the cessation of functional cultural life, but interestingly, in his classic study of suicide published exactly a century ago, Emile Durkheim drew a link between life based on illusion and the individual act of suicide. In cultures that remove ethical, social, and physical constraints, he maintained, "a thirst arises for novelties, unfamiliar pleasures, nameless sensations, all of which lose their savor once known. . . . Reality in this state of crisis is abandoned to illusion" (256). In many ways, our culture's thirst for sensation without limit and our own abandonment of reality for illusion may betoken the same self-destructive end for us collectively that Durkheim describes on the individual level. What we will tolerate on television has been pushed to its outer limits, driving reality out almost entirely. Talk shows give us glimpses of what are purported to be real people with representative problems from which we can learn to live our own lives. But if an episode of Ricki Lake's show, say, were to be placed into a time capsule and discovered in a millennium, would it be anything but a grossly distorted reflection of American social reality in the 1990s?

Having said that, however, we must also acknowledge that this dangerous cultural tendency of ours cannot be laid entirely at television's door. Rather, it is the result of the unhappy confluence of available technology, historical events, and other changes, including shifts from a producer economy to a consumption-based economy, the countercultural attack by the radical left during the social upheavals of the 1960s, and the backlash of the "new conservatism" underscored by ongoing ideological debates over such things as relativity versus absolutism. Lacking any of these factors, TV's toxic talk would probably not exist. The producers of the current crop of tawdry talk programs—indeed, all of the controlling parties of commercial television—are partially right when they argue disingenuously that their programs merely reflect public taste and demand. The question then becomes, how did such taste take shape? Certainly television played a major role by spreading, exacerbating, oversimplifying, and misconstruing the social forces at work. It also got us used to and excited about our easy access to continuous entertainment.

Arguably a most significant factor has been the head-on collision of middle-class Americans' expectations and economic circumstances. Ironically, given the consumer-oriented nature of television and our transformation into a nation of consumers, the present generation is probably the first one, at least in the postwar period, not to match or top their parents' standard of living. At the same time that buying power has shrunk, our illusions as a culture have become more extravagant. As our infotainment sources bombard us with lavish images of the lifestyles of the rich and famous, of sports figures earning millions of dollars for a single season of play, of computer geniuses who control the world (real and virtual), we expect reality to live up to our images and fantasies about it, as pointed out in such early social criticisms as Daniel Boorstin's *The Image* and Philip Slater's *The Pursuit of Loneliness: American Culture at the Breaking Point.* We look for quick fixes to whatever prevents us from attaining the good life, even as we lose economic ground. This paradox has led to real anger on the part of the middle-class wage earner.

Trashy television talk programs are attractive and comforting to these individuals because the programs typically showcase people who, in class and condition, are lower than they are on the social ladder, the diametric opposite of the celebrated rich and famous. The middle class—those who tune in regularly but would themselves never divulge private matters of this sort on television—get a laugh and feel better about their own class circumstances. However unsavory such behavior may seem, it's really not so unusual. Very often, we benchmark our own experiences against and take solace from the plight of those less fortunate—or, in this case, less socially respectable—than ourselves. Of course, the shows also appeal to the "lower-class" audience, who sees itself mirrored in the shows' guests and their revelations. For their part, the "disreputable" underclass have little to lose by appearing on such programs, and at least they can console themselves with the fact that America is listening to them now, however mockingly.

Not so typical and far more disturbing, however, is the fact that many middle-class viewers have come to identify with the underclass who bare all on the talk-game shows. In *The Unheavenly City Revisited*, Edward Banfield writes that lower-class individuals generally "lack a concern for the future, a sense of control over their fate, and self-discipline; they prefer 'action' to work, are insensitive to the value of property and do not value education. . . . They live for the moment and do not engage in community work or care about issues confronting the larger social world around them" (61-62). The middle class, by contrast, has traditionally subscribed to a fixed value system derived in part from Puritan religion, in part from emulation of the upper class. The idea of delayed gratification and of storing up treasures now to be used hereafter are part of the Protestant ethic, as is their code of civil behavior. Social and economic success, like the eternal rewards of Heaven, were to be earned through hard work, industry, use of one's talents, reticence, self-control, humility, modesty, and adherence to the cardinal virtues, notably honesty. This system worked so well, of course, because it happily combined the promise of eternal reward with the very practical rewards of material success in the here and now. For its part, the upper class taught the middle class the professional and personal uses of formal education, practicable definitions of social decorum, and the view of personal property as sacrosanct. Recently, Richard Bushman wrote about the old belief in proper conduct as the hallmark of the middle class: "One might not be able to live in the same neighborhood as an Astor or Biddle, but it was nevertheless possible through diligent effort to lay claim to an equal place in 'respect-able' society" (20). These beliefs and behaviors formed the foundation of the American Dream, as popularized in the novels of Horatio Alger, and became the formula for success in a land of opportunity.

Now all of that is regarded as next to useless as American corporate structures daily betray the value system that the middle class was founded upon. In her 1995 book, Gertrude Himmelfarb termed this phenomenon the "demoralization of society," referring both to the psychic state of Americans and to their attitude toward conventional middle-class morality. Himmelfarb argues that virtues are "intransient," whereas values can be followed, ignored, or changed. Moreover, one can claim to subscribe to a value system without actually following it behaviorally. On the other hand, there can be no disjunction between true morality and behavior. Many contemporary Americans feel that these old social verities no longer pay dividends in crassly materialistic America. Big businesses sell off American factories and other high-employment workplaces, and the richest Americans are paying a smaller percentage of the nation's taxes than ever before. As a result of corporate decisions, many middle-class people are losing jobs or taking part-time jobs with no job security or health and pension benefits. Unions have been in retreat since the Reagan era, and working people are frightened.[7] Even those who still believe in the American Dream and who are "grooming" (that term itself is troubling) themselves for success subscribe to other, more superficial, formulas than the ones characterized by Horatio Alger. In his novels, it was a combination of "luck and pluck" that enabled the hero to succeed. Today, rather, the emphasis is on a kind of national lottery—luck (something over which we have no control) being the more important factor. It's not what you know or who you are that counts. We end up giving up on the hard work involved in controlling external forces and instead rely on impression management, a search for pleasure, and a solipsistic effort at feeling good and ensuring self-esteem. Hard work *at* a job is not a guarantee of upward mobility, and so we work *on* our own images instead.

In keeping with this idea of image over substance is the prevalence of the therapeutic model of social behavior over the old ethical models. The new quick-fix model offers preposterous optimism in its approaches to human suffering and human failings. No one has done the unforgivable; everyone can be "saved" as long as they can get with the program. This program, aimed at troubled and addicted people, is widely available in support groups, self-help books, and most pervasively, on talk-television programs. Pop psychologists come on offering caricatures of psychotherapy and simplistic programmatic "advice" to the troubled: Get in touch with your feelings, follow a 12-step program, go looking for your inner child. In his posthumously published book, *The Revolt of the Elites and the Betrayal of Democracy*, Christopher Lasch accurately asserted, "We do children a terrible disservice . . . by showering them with undeserved approval. The kind of reassurance they need comes only with a growing ability to meet impersonal standards of competence. . . . Self-respect cannot be conferred; it has to be earned. Current therapeutic and pedagogical practice, all 'empathy' and 'understanding,' hopes to manufacture self-respect without the risk" (206-08).

Clearly growing up and maturing as social creatures in a social framework is hard work, and the more we move away from the old values, work ethic, and social interaction itself, the more unaccustomed to hard work we become. Instead, we want risk-free self-respect because it's easy—like watching television—and therefore it is not surprising that casually redemptive advice has taken the place of conventional and lengthy psychotherapy, not to mention moral judgment and blame. Victimization and/or illness are cited as the major causes of bad actions to the exclusion of all other reasons for negative behavior, including free choice. As Abt and McGurrin discussed in their 1991 article on the politics of addiction counseling, no matter what you've done to yourself or others, no matter how irresponsibly you have behaved, you can be reborn (in some cases, right there on television) and get in touch with the innocent child within, who has remained unsullied by the worst of your sins. The wounds of life need not be fatal.

This final article of faith caricatures the old hopeful pragmatism that Americans have loved so much. Despite empirical evidence to the contary, we cling to the populist belief that people can overcome most circumstances of nature, nurture, and class, but we have culturally redefined the means of overcoming them. Instead of hard work and decorous behavior, we now believe in the quick fix. We can "get in touch with ourselves" (whatever that means!) with the aid of Oprah's or Geraldo's "after care," along with a variety of supposedly self-improving exercises, techniques, assurances of success, and of course, the support of millions of viewers. The sociologist or, for that matter, the humanist, who is rarely or never on these programs, might point out the importance of social conditions and complex environmental factors, including law, bureaucracy, and economics in understanding and addressing individual problems. However, it is the pop therapist who continues to win the day, preaching the pseudo-gospel of freedom from social constraint and elevating the inner child to god-like status. And on the other end of the camera are the spectators of this "therapy," the consumers of entertainment who are led to believe that there is social benefit in what they are watching and who rationalize their own eavesdropping by asserting their openmindedness and supportiveness, even though most viewers are neither. The genre itself is fraught with deception—a lack of acknowledgment of the fundamental "inaccessibility" of people in their innermost thoughts and motives, a lack of respect for people in the incessant asking of "suggestive" questions under pretense of "concern" for the person being questioned. Whereas, in the Victorian print era, people were considered "closed books" with their own inner life, private matters and secrets, the electronic age, with its constantly changing and invasive images, has made therapy a public event, a spectator sport.

This do-your-own-thing philosophy can be partially traced back to the liberal 1960s, which also indirectly provide a clue to current social attitudes. At that time, radical activists and intellectuals believed that the social ills of the nation, if not the world, could be fixed, but first a wholesale rejection of cultural standards had to take place. The point of view of the power elite (the Establishment) had to be repudiated, replaced with a cultural tolerance for any and all points of view, the prototype of today's cultural relativity. When, a decade later, that social experiment was deemed a failure and the old problems remained intact or were even exacerbated, a vacuum was left, and into it rushed two potent forces—right-wing politicians and the supposedly liberal media. (As we shall see in chapter 6, the cozy partnerships between conservative government and the controllers of the media have grown ever stronger and have now reached crisis proportions.) They brought with them a kind of schizophrenic cultural reaction. On the one hand, the liberal television media carried on the cultural relativism of the 1960s, eventually giving us the talk shows, which depend largely upon the notion that we must listen to and tolerate deviance of all kinds. Woody Allen's character jokes in the movie *Manhattan Murder Mystery* that the possible wife-killer living next door to him is "living an alternative life style" in a nonjudgmental, culturally diverse New York; but that thinking is the serious basis of discussion on the talk shows. On the other hand, the appeal of the radical right in politics and even extremist cults in our culture stems in large measure perhaps from our attempts to escape the "freedom" from standards and to retreat into certainty with the help of censuring groups.

Talk TV has provided the perfect bridge between these opposing viewpoints. While showcasing deviance, talk shows also deliberately incite conservative, reactionary feelings of bigotry and self-righteousness in the middle class. A pregnant welfare mother collecting government subsidies for her eight illegitimate children and boasting about it on television provokes at least a couple of reactions in the average middle-class viewer: amusement at the spectacle of a boastful social misfit and contempt, even hatred, for this living cause of excessive taxation. When the host of the program asks provocative questions eliciting responses that are intended to arouse the audience's ire, the confluence of these two streams becomes complete.

At the heart of the entire enterprise, of course, is the selling of commercial time and its predictable end result—consumption. In his essay "But Now a Word from Our Sponsor," James Twitchell observes that "modern selling is not about trading information, as it was in the 19th century, as much as about creating an infotainment culture with sufficient allure to enable other messages— commercials—to get through" (68). One of the more basic problems associated with these shows was pointed out by *The Washington Post*'s media critic, Tom Shales, at the end of the *Oprah* show on which he and Abt appeared to discuss talk shows. Shales was asked by Ms. Winfrey what he thought was wrong with talk shows specifically and television in general. He replied that he would like to see more intelligent people given attention and a forum, meaning that reasonable, critical thinking is rarely showcased on television for the obvious reason that such thinking does not serve any commercial interest on the part of sponsors or producers. As a culture, we are so habituated to the modus operandi of television that we have largely ceased to question the appropiateness of interrupting what appears to be real life for commercial messages or even the meaning of those messages. To use an example cited earlier, an episode of Maury Povich's program featured the surviving member of a set of anorexic twins, the other having died recently. The painfully emaciated survivor at one point begs the audience not to start dieting because she and her dead twin did just that and then couldn't stop. Following this heartbreaking plea, Maury breaks for a commercial on, of all subjects, Quick Weight Loss products!

All of us—producers and owners, advertisers, consumers, even government—are only too happy to conspire in the commercial ends of television generally and talk TV in particular. "Commercials have worked—with success—toward revision of many traditional tenets of our society," writes Erik Barnouw in *The Sponsor*. "Reverence for nature (reality) has been replaced by a determination to process it (to consume it). Thrift has been replaced by the duty to buy. The work ethic has been replaced by the consumption ethic. 'Conspicuous consumption,' once considered an unworthy tendency of the leisure classes (Veblen) has been sanctified and democratized. . . . Modesty has been exorcised with help from the sexual sell. Restraint of ego has lost standing. . . . Self-love is consecrated ritual" (98). These observations strike at the very heart of the talk-show game—loss of modesty and restraint, incessant chatter about "self-love" and "self-esteem," happiness at all costs.

Ultimately, however, the happiest parties will be those who directly profit the most: the corporate owners and sponsors and a laissez-faire government that can count on their "partners," if only to help them finance reelection, not to fill the tax coffers for the greater good. Talk shows are perfectly illustrative of the two major forces in the world today. According to Benjamin Barber's work *Jihad vs. McWorld*, "Jihad pursues a bloody politics of identity, McWorld a bloodless economics of profit" (7). The personal conflict of warring families and parochial ethnicities ensures the programs' appeal in an age of impersonal global commerce where we are only consumers. Producers and distributors package this emotional display as they coolly consider their audience share and subsequent revenues.

As noted in a 1986 *Time* cover story, "Pop culture is, after all, the culture of the free market: Heather Locklear and Prince and Chuck Norris are all laissez-faire by-products. Only in a wildly unregulated society could such beings have a ready means of becoming rich and famous. As a practical matter, too, only capitalists have both the necessary cash and unembarrassed eagerness to please" (69). In the decade since that article appeared, the capitalists have become even more eager to please, regardless of the social cost, and government more eager to let them by deregulating even further. Hence, for all of their apparent disagreement, both liberal and conservative elements are operating together within this social vacuum to further their own interests and agendas, cynically selling out the American people in the process. The next chapter considers more closely this wedding of governmental and corporate forces, bringing about political changes that have made possible, among other things, the growth and greater toxicity of talk TV.

Notes

1. For a good source on the changing theatrical tastes of the Greeks and Romans, see Elizabeth Burns, *Theatricality: A Study of Convention in the Theatre and in Social Life* (New York: Harper, 1973).

2. For a good overview of frames and their relevance to culture, see Erving Goffman, *Frame Analysis: An Essay on the Organization of Experience* (Cambridge: Harvard University Press, 1974).

3. Some particularly good overviews on the transforming power of the "Age of Television" include Frank Mankiewicz and Joel Swerdlow, *Remote Control: Television and the Manipulation of American Life* (New York: Ballantine Books, 1978); Ian Mitroff and Warren Bennis, *The Unreality Industry: The Deliberate Manufacturing of Falsehood and What It Is Doing to Our Lives* (New York: Birch Lane, 1989); Michael Parenti, *Make-Believe Media: The Politics of Entertainment* (New York: St. Martin's, 1992).

4. The power of television to influence public opinion and rivet the nation on a single happening was perhaps first evidenced with the televising of Senator Joseph McCarthy's Permanent Subcommittee in the spring of 1954. Few of us who watched and listened will forget the Senator yelling, "Point of Order! Point of Order," and Joseph Welch, the lawyer representing the Army, admonishing the Senator in the moment that proved McCarthy's undoing: "Have you no sense of decency, sir, at long last?" Of course, the famous televising of the Nixon/Kennedy debates years later changed politics from the "substantive" coverage of issues debated to the "image" of the candidate on television. Many of those who heard the debates on radio thought Nixon won, while the majority of those who saw the debate on television regarded Kennedy as the winner.

5. In 1983 the National Commission on Excellence in Education warned that "Our Nation Is at Risk." This was even before the "Oprah-ization of America," the decade of toxic talk that we are discussing in this book. Educator Jonathan Kozol in *Illiterate America* (New York: Doubleday, 1985) states that "a third of our nation cannot read" the words of his book (3). Many of these very people are the heaviest watchers of television generally and talk television specifically. MIT economist Lester Thurow in *Head to Head: The Coming Economic Battle Among Japan, Europe, and America* (New York: Warner, 1993) warns about the imminent decline in America's power because of slipping literacy and intellectual development. Comparative international exams reveal that Americans at all age and class levels know less than citizens abroad in the advanced industrial countries (we have also watched the most television for the most years). Skilled people are the only sustainable competitive advantage in the global economy, where land barriers

and dependence on local raw materials are not as important as communicable knowledge and where a nation's wealth is no longer only measured in raw materials and factories. Products can be developed in one place and manufactured in another anywhere in the world because of faster transportation and shipping, but it is a nation's brainpower that is its stable product (52, 154, 274).

6. See especially Stanton Peele, *The Meaning of Addiction: Compulsive Experience and Its Interpretation* (Lexington: Lexington/D. C. Heath, 1985); Daniel Boorstin, *The Image: A Guide to Pseudo-Events in America* (New York: Atheneum, 1961); and Christopher Lasch, *The Culture of Narcissism: American Life in an Age of Diminishing Expectations* (New York: Norton, 1979) and *The Revolt of the Elites and the Betrayal of Democracy* (New York: Norton, 1995).

7. For a good overview of these fears, see the book by *The Philadelphia Inquirer*'s investigative reporters Donald Barlett and James Steele, *America: What Went Wrong?* (Kansas City: Andrews & McMeel, 1992).

6

Talking Business and Playing Monopoly

Freedom of the press (or any medium of speech) is guaranteed only to those who own one.

—A. J. Liebling,
The New Yorker May 14, 1960

We're giving the American people what they want. If you want to give people what you think they need, go into public broadcasting.

—Tom Murphy, president of Cap Cities,
before the purchase of ABC in 1984

The supposed explosion of media outlets via cable and fiber optics has created an incentive for government to excuse itself from the messy business of regulation. . . . New media monopolies are coming into existence without so much as a glance from federal authorities who once upon a time would have been screaming for antitrust action.

—Benjamin Barber,
Jihad vs. McWorld (1995)

To promote competition and reduce regulation in order to secure lower prices and higher quality services for American telecommunications consumers.

—Introductory words of the
Telecommunications Act of 1996
(Public Law 104-104, February 8, 1996)

Geraldo: The program is called "Grudge Match," a series of confrontations between warring "lovers." The first contestants up are two women fighting over a man. They are white, he black. His name is Cliff.

119

Geraldo gets things going with a probing, pointed question to the women: "Are either of you sure you want this S.O.B.?"

"They know what they want," Cliff answers for them, proud and leering.

Geraldo redirects his question to one of the women, Stacy. He wants to know what attracts her to Cliff. Not to be outdone in the directness department, Stacy demonstrates. "Right there," she asserts, pointing at his crotch. The scandalized audience lets forth with oohs and aahs, loving every minute of this display.

A few similar encounters later, and a concerned Geraldo is ready to offer them help in the form of a "therapist," one Linda Barberella, C.S.W., who is variously identified in the chyrons as "Family Counselor" and "Advice Columnist." Whatever "C.S.W." refers to is never explained. Geraldo's first question to her says it all: "Have I created enough for you?" Created.

"This is family therapy at its zenith," she replies. "I think there's hope." What therapy? What family? Hope for what? She doesn't say.

The host, the guests, the studio audience, and the world watching are now given a view from the zenith of family therapy. "We all have to take responsibility for our actions," Linda says seriously, professionally. "I think there's real caring here. Communication can start."

But before anyone can start communicating, Geraldo communicates. "Let's take a break." It's 4:48 P.M., and only twelve minutes remain in the therapeutic portion of the program. The advertisers now communicate for three and a half minutes.

That business done—or perhaps better to say the real *business done—Linda Barberella, C.S.W., returns to communicate more professional advice to the lovelorn. "It'll be greater to have the cake and not the crumb. . . . It's better to have a girlfriend sometimes than to have a boyfriend. . . . More self-esteem, ladies!" That last bit of advice is the most profound and helpful. Heads nod in agreement across America.*

The healing having begun, the ever-caring Geraldo gets the last word, his two cents' worth, as he puts it. "Let me know how it works out," he asks them, and then to the camera, "Stay tuned." A final break for business, and it's over. (July 1995)

In an analysis for *The Philadelphia Inquirer* (August 6, 1995) of the recent network-television acquisitions by Disney and Westinghouse, Andrew Cassel argues that the public erroneously believes these moves are the work of "Masters of the Universe playing dice with the world" or modern-day robber barons monopolistically cornering markets. Rather, Cassel concludes, Michael Eisner (Disney), Rupert Murdoch (Fox), Sumner Redstone (Viacom), and Ted Turner (Turner Broadcasting) are only fashioning "fragile creations," which, unlike mines or factories, are "built on myths and images—a.k.a. entertainment—and on the unenforceable loyalty of tens of millions of consumers. As new forms of communications and entertainment technology have emerged over the last decade, the ability of the old TV networks to assemble a mass audience at will has been chipped away. . . . The shelves are bigger, with many more products competing for consumers' attention" (D1, D5). We believe, however, that popular perception has a lot more truth in it than Cassel's "expert" analysis. As we've suggested throughout this book, it is precisely our "myths and images" that frame our culture and, in an earlier industrial America, formed the bedrock for a vibrant, competitive, and optimistic democracy. Moreover, we do not think it entirely fortuitous that the decade of toxic-talk television coincides with the decade of increasing deregulation of the media resulting in the final passage of the Telecommunications Act of 1996.

It goes practically without saying that the nature of American industry and the basis of American wealth and influence have changed markedly in this century—from the control of manufactured products, commodities, and natural resources in the Gilded Age to information and services in our time. For example, not a single computer is manufactured entirely in the United States, but we are the world leaders in computer applications and sales for that matter. If we export our high-tech expertise to the world, it's not in the form of hardware (which would have been the stock-in-trade of the old robber barons) but symbolic culture that is communicated as the product of media technology, as well as the knowledge of how to use technology in education, medicine, urban design, and, most of all, telecommunications. Thus, however intangible the assets of the communications Goliaths may appear compared to John D. Rockefeller's oil, Andrew Carnegie's steel, and Henry Ford's Model-T, they are for our time every bit as lucrative, appealing, socially transforming, monopolistic, and influential. Hardly "fragile creations," the myths and images of American culture stand as sturdy symbols of the nation's contemporary spirit.

Of course, no single corporation currently controls all the mass media and, at least indirectly its cultural messages, in the United States, but the direction in which things are moving is not promising. "If mergers, acquisitions, and takeovers continue at the present rate," Ben Bagdikian observed in his 1992 book, *Media Monopoly*, "one massive firm will be in virtual control of all major media by the 21st century. . . . Today despite more than 25,000 outlets in the U.S., 23 corporations control most of the business in daily newspapers, magazines, television, books, and motion pictures" (4). In the few years since he made that assertion, even fewer corporate entities run the media business, and we appear to be well on the way to the "one massive firm" that Bagdikian predicted. As for the "unenforceable loyalty" of consumers, that ceases to be a problem when power is concentrated in so few hands. The audience will eat up what is served up, and as long as the illusion of choice is maintained under the guise of free enterprise, few will complain. Of course, this illusion is maintained by the burgeoning cable field and the decline in the original three networks' total control over broadcasting. More channels don't necessarily mean more real diversity or choices for the consumer.

Again, as Bagdikian points out, regardless of the specific people in control over however many "different" channels we see, "They [the media moguls] have shared values. Those values are reflected in the emphasis of their news and popular culture. They are the primary shapers of American public opinion about events and their meaning. And through that, and their organization in large powerful corporate units, they are a major influence on government" (10). Call it the commercialization of culture through the media. In other words, program content, politics, and economics are inextricably intertwined. These forces were held in check when no company (network) was permitted to own more than seven radio and seven television stations. Under the media's push for deregulation these political limits have all but been erased. When Fred Friendly resigned as president of CBS News in 1966 because the network didn't want to cancel an episode of *I Love Lucy* for a critical Senate hearing on Vietnam (for commercial reasons), we saw the beginning of the "accountants" or "bean counters" making content or programming policies.

What is not so easily recognized by the viewing public is that many of these supposed "competitors" are owned by the few media conglomerates. (Paradoxically, it can even be argued that when there were only the three major networks competing head to head, they could take more risks with quality programming.) That all of these supposed choices, while possessing different corporate names, are concentrated among an increasingly smaller handful of powerful media controllers goes generally unknown and unprotested despite the almost daily examples that fill the headlines.[1] As we write, Turner Broadcasting was acquired by Time Warner. Although Sumner Redstone and Frank Biondi control Viacom, John Malone, owner of QVC and the TCI cable system serving about 14 million subscribers, was trying to buy Viacom. Multimedia's Donald Sbarra is awaiting a pending buyout by John Curley's Gannett. Disney acquired Cap Cities/ABC, CBS was bought by Westinghouse, and NBC merged with General Electric in 1986 (Carter D1). That leaves no independent television networks among the big three. The summer of 1996 brought the announcement of Westinghouse's merging with Infinity Cable due to the relaxation of rules against television and radio cross-ownership (Cassel A19). In December of 1996, the government removed the last regulatory obstacle and agreed to the $3.9 billion merger, creating the nation's largest radio group. The new group will operate 79 radio stations in 17 markets (Aversa, "Giant" C1). In addition to the obvious game of Monopoly being played in the media industry, there's also the game of musical chairs, with each round leaving fewer chairs in the business.

In the previous chapter, we considered the question of how we came to this pass as a culture, what made it possible for the toxic-talk programs to take root and flourish. Here we again deal with the question of origins, only the focus is shifted to government bureaucracies and corporations that have worked together to limit competition in the name of free markets. As the editors of *The New York Times* suggest in "Let's Get Big: Media Merger Mania— Is the Public Served?" (September 2, 1995) the real reason for the acquisition frenzy during the summer of 1995 was the desire to reduce financial risks, and the safest bets at the moment seem to be the inexpensively produced toxic-talk shows. The writers correctly predicted that this thinking would bring about a new set of "Geraldo clones." More important, they stated that these deals would not have happened without major changes in regulatory policy that made networks more attractive to investors. "For years, Hollywood studios lobbied Washington to keep the syndication rule because they did not want the networks to horn in on their business. With the rule about to expire, the studios are solving their problem by buying the networks" (18). Moreover, by eliminating the prime-time access rule and allowing the networks to show their programs in the 7 to 8 P.M. time slot, the FCC has added hundreds of millions of dollars to the value of CBS, NBC, and ABC. To say the least, these developments do not augur well for the future of American media and, ultimately, American diversity of opinion.

As corporate and governmental forces combine to limit the voices in the marketplace, they have effectively created within our democratic state a privileged oligarchy that, because of the nature of its business, is far more dangerous in the long run than having only a handful of companies controlling the sales of oil or steel or cars or, for that matter, three networks controlling television. It is more dangerous because what these few communications companies influence and profit from is nothing short of American cultural consciousness through news, information, and entertainment, all of which have been rolled into a single amorphous whole for our amusement and which threaten both our constitutionally defined freedoms and our very minds. Numerous commentators have made these arguments. Like Bagdikian, Dennis Mazzocco, for instance, notes in *Networks of Power* that "the media monopoly of 1992 consisted of 20 communication conglomerates. In 1983, more than 50 such conglomerates existed" (143). Mazzocco also suggests that media executives are able to hide behind their First Amendment rights in order to prevent greater citizen participation in their corporate buyouts. These executives also have the money to buy up the airwaves and print outlets and the power to influence government policies in ways inconceivable to the average person. In *The Sponsor* (1978), Erik Barnouw warned that the very media being controlled also affect our knowledge of the media barons' activities, along with our ability to analyze their intentions clearly. After all, we get our information from these corporate wheelers and dealers, mostly through television, a medium that is not conducive to careful analysis. "The air of authenticity is everywhere," Barnouw writes. "Operating on the borderline between fact and fiction, producers aim at "showmanship. . . . Disentangling fact from fiction may be almost impossible for most viewers" (104).

To borrow Paul Fussell's well-chosen book subtitle, the "Dumbing of America," much of it being carried out deliberately in the name of profits, undermines both our ability to think and, therefore, all of our democratic institutions. Easily consumed entertainment or news that seeks to entertain lulls our critical faculties as it shapes attitudes, beliefs, and values. Ironically (or perhaps better to say tragically), this movement toward mind-numbing diversion could not come at a worse time. Owing to the high-tech nature of modern life and the information "explosion," Americans will need to develop *greater* reasoning and analytical skills if they hope to make it in the world—make it both as individuals in terms of earning power and as a nation in competition in the "global marketplace."

Even when radio broadcasting was in its infancy, there was much concern that powerful corporations or individuals would gain control of the influential medium. The first station to go on the air was Westinghouse Electric and Manufacturing Company's KDKA in Pittsburgh in 1920, and it set off an immediate explosion. Hundreds of entrepreneurs began building stations, and by 1922, 400 licenses had been issued. By 1927 that number nearly doubled, with 90 being operated by educational institutions, and the Federal Radio Commission came into being as a watchdog agency. Through much of the first decade of radio broadcasting, programs were commercial free. When David Sarnoff of RCA first proposed the idea of a radio network in 1922, he envisioned it as a nonprofit public service, with no advertising allowed. (Sarnoff, incidentally, expected his company's profits to come from the sale of radios, not airtime.) By the time sponsors did enter the picture, they provided minimal subsidies to support the broadcasts and were regarded generally as patrons of the arts. One sponsor was featured for an entire program, and among the earliest were AT&T and Revlon cosmetics. Still, the growing presence of these agents, combined with the recognized "power" of the medium itself, led many to be concerned about the effect of radio on the public welfare.[2]

To counter its potential threat to the public airwaves (and, through them, the public consciousness), Congress passed the Communications Act of 1934, creating a permanent regulatory agency, the Federal Communications Commission (FCC). Under this liberal New Deal policy of government intervention, the standard for licensing radio stations was "the public interest, convenience, and necessity." This somewhat slippery phrase was borrowed from public-utility legislation recognizing the different and higher standards that should apply to industries that monopolistically supplied critical services to the general public. In the case of the FCC, the Constitutional protection of freedom of speech for broadcasters was subordinated to the public's welfare. As Kenneth Creech notes in his book *Electronic Media Law and Regulation*, "[F]reedom of speech was to apply to speech deemed to be in the public interest. It was not that the speech of broadcasters was to be protected, as much as it was the right of the audience to be protected from certain forms of speech" (56). In keeping with this idea, in 1949 the government imposed what was termed the Fairness Doctrine, which directed station licensees to provide an opportunity for contrasting viewpoints. No such doctrine governed the print media because it would have been considered a violation of free speech and because radio and TV frequencies are limited. (Anyone can start a newspaper—at least theoretically.) Thus, the airwaves were always considered a realm apart with regard to the First Amendment, more a public trust like the utilities rather than a democratic forum. The recent ruling against the Communications Decency Act (part of the Telecommunications Act of 1996), which would have regarded the Internet as something akin more to television and radio than the press, illustrates the assumption that radio and television must be treated differently as their frequencies are limited and can therefore be regulated in the public interest. The federal judges in Philadelphia suggested in their decision that Internet was "mass speech" and could not be so regulated (Stets 1E).

Although early licensing practices and standards were developed as protective measures, before long the lucrative media industry found ways to exploit, circumvent, and weaken these protections. The cause of this erosion of standards was clearly the commercial interests, particularly in the form of advertising revenues. By "renting out" the public airwaves, corporate America learned that it could exchange a token FCC licensing fee for billions of dollars in sales. This sponsor-supported system offered a clear pattern to be applied in the age of television, which was introduced in the late 1940s. By then, that idea was a given, and from its inception, the new medium was dominated by commercial interests.

For its part, government has also been confusingly contradictory in its policies toward this mega-business over the course of the past sixty years. After decades of close government scrutiny, the Nixon administration began simultaneously to deregulate and reregulate television. The move with the greatest consequences was the introduction in 1970 of the financial interest and syndication rules (fin-syn). Designed essentially to loosen the networks' monopolistic grip over the airwaves and to promote diversity among TV producers, fin-syn prohibited the networks from having a financial stake in the entertainment series they ran. Consequently, they were compelled to rely on Hollywood studios to produce the programs they broadcast. The networks' financial interest in syndicated programs sold to affiliate stations was also limited by these regulations, which unintentionally fueled the growth of syndicators and independent stations. Thus, while reducing the concentration of power in the networks' hands, the government also brought about the creation of vast corporate power entities with interests in radio, TV, cable, print, and entertainment productions over the past twenty-five years. The fin-syn rules expired in November 1995. Indeed they had already been radically weakened over the years, and the anticipation of their eventual total demise helped set off the frenzied acquisition activity that took place in the summer of 1995 by such giants as Disney, Westinghouse, and Time Warner (Covington 3-19).

In fact, deregulatory efforts had begun to intensify during the Reagan administration, weakening the FCC's oversight function and giving more power to the media giants. (Even the size of the commission was reduced in 1982 from seven to five members.) In 1981, the FCC eliminated rules that required radio stations to ascertain community needs in their city of license by formally surveying community leaders and the general public and generating appropriate programming. In 1984, such standards for television stations were also dropped. And, in 1985, the FCC dropped "must-carry rules," and reversed the long-cherished Fairness Doctrine, asserting that the multiplicity of voices in the marketplace represented a reasonable substitute. Just how this was so when the corporate entities became more and more monolithic was never explained. Other changes included increasing the term of license from three to seven years and eliminating requirements that stations keep program logs and guidelines for the amount of commercial time. Moreover the number of stations that a single group or individual could own increased dramatically in 1985. Mazzocco cites that year, the one in which Capital Cities acquired ABC, as a watershed year in the road toward the creation of the giant media cartels (143). The old "Rule of 7," introduced in 1953 and restricting ownership to seven AM stations, seven FM stations, and seven television stations, became the "Rule of 12." Cross ownership of broadcast stations and print media remained prohibited until the Telecommunications Act of 1996 removed the restrictions against cross ownership. It revised the limitations in a radio market to not more than 50% of the stations in some radio markets and virtually eliminated restrictions on the number of television stations that a person or entity could directly or indirectly control by increasing the national audience permissibly reached to 35% (Telecommunications Act of 1996 Sec. 202, "Broadcast Ownership," 110, Stat 110).

As journalist Ken Auletta has noted, nevertheless, until recently few outwardly challenged the idea that the FCC had the right and responsibility to monitor the airwaves in the public interest. Then, under Reagan's first FCC chairman, Mark S. Fowler, that assumption crumbled, and Fowler saw TV as just another business, "a toaster with pictures," with the marketplace determining the winners and losers (32). Likewise, Kenneth Creech has argued that the new view at the FCC at the time corresponded with Reagan's campaign promise to get government off the backs of the people, but in reality, he managed only to get government "off the backs of the broadcasters" (75). Once the media giants moved in—replete with lobbyists, money, and the power of the media itself over the politicians' images—there was not to be any turning back.

The current laissez-faire attitude of government toward big business, notably the entertainment business, is perhaps the prime reason for the media mergers and buyouts we've been witnessing. Washington has given a tremendous deregulatory shrug of its shoulders. In 1994, the ownership "Rule of 12" established in 1985 was scrapped, and companies could own up to forty radio stations and twelve television stations. Then, in August 1995, the House of Representatives approved a bill that would radically rewrite the nation's communications laws for the first time in the six decades since the dawn of radio broadcasting and the creation of the FCC. Eventually the bill became the Telecommunications Act of 1996. The new law passed by the Republican-led 104th Congress lifted restrictions on media cross-ownership, allowing single companies to own TV stations that reach up to 35% of the U.S. (up from the 25% current limit) and as many radio stations as it wants (the previous limit was forty stations).[3] It would also allow radio stations, phone companies, network TV and cable stations, and newspaper companies to buy each other out, even in the same market. Westinghouse, for example, now owns 80 radio stations (Cassel A19). The result, of course, could be the creation of impregnable monoliths, vertically integrated corporate entities that would provide *all* of the information that the American people receive from *all* media.

Such vertical integrations are hardly new creations. John D. Rockefeller's Standard Oil, Sam Goldwyn's movie studios, and the old AT&T all built top to bottom, source to consumer companies of this sort. But as Kevin Maney points out in his article "Media Firms Shift to Gain Product Control" (*USA Today*, September 14, 1995), the earlier "airtight vertical organizations . . . ran afoul of antitrust laws and were broken up. But vertical integration has gotten new life thanks to changes in media and communications regulations and an increasingly competitive atmosphere" (B1, B2). Maney concludes that no one really knows whether these organizations will hurt consumers and that, according to unnamed analysts, "consumers should see little effect on prices or offerings" with a few competing corporations of this kind. This optimistic view of the new monopolies is dangerously myopic. After all, what consumers *see* is not the point. It's what they're getting from homogenized, all-controlling corporations that threaten the American public. Ben Bagdikian argues that "when the same corporations expand their control over many different kinds of media, they speak glowingly of producing richer public choices in news and entertainment. But the experience has been that the common control of different media makes those media more alike than ever. Movies become like television series. Cable, once thought to be a fundamental alternative to programs on commercial television but now under control of companies also in television and other media, is increasingly an imitation of commercial television" (7).

Because of the recent easing of time lengths permitted for a single commercial, many cable stations now air half hour and hour infomercials, another blurring of frames, this time between information and commercials. Twitchell puts it this way: "Programs are the scheduled interruptions of marketing bulletins. . . . Thanks to the remote-control wand and the coaxial (soon to be fiber optic) cable, commercials will disappear. They will become the programming" (76-77). As Bagdikian also points out, after cable deregulation, in the name of opening competition and product development, cable rates charged by dominant firms rose as much as 50% faster than production costs (7). A June 28, 1996, article in *The Philadelphia Inquirer* stated that under current changes in FCC rules, recently ordered by Congress, individual customers are prevented from asking the government to review rate increases for expanded basic cable (Aversa D1). Hence, when a few companies control all of the information and entertainment we are exposed to and when smaller companies—minority voices, as it were—find it all but impossible to enter the marketplace, free speech becomes a meaningless exercise and the customer pays more.

While the 1970s fin-syn rules were enacted with the best of intentions, they actually brought about the creation of near monopolistic syndicators and Hollywood production companies with more power because of their wide-flung empires over the entire flow of information we receive than the old networks. The current deregulation frenzy threatens the multiplicity of voices as never before in the nation's history. Addressing the problems involved in appropriate regulation by almost totally deregulating and allowing tremendous corporate concentrations of media power in the $700 billion industry seems at the very least, irresponsible and misguided, at worst, representative of a short-sighted collusion between government and industry. As one analyst has noted, "the most important factor precipitating this dramatic consolidation in the entertainment industry might be the laissez-faire attitude toward big business that prevails in Washington" (Groves C1). The opening words of the Telecommunications Act of 1996 quoted as an epigram to this chapter represent a strange contradiction. Deregulation has clearly not, in the past, ensured more competition, higher quality programming, or lower prices. America's history with unfettered vertical monopolies should have taught us all the pressing need for legislative oversight and judicial antitrust action to counter huge powerful oligarchies.

Interestingly, these deregulatory moves are themselves often bipartisan in outlook, each group justifying its decision ideologically. The right, while complaining of the dumbing down of American education, tries to kill off "elitist" PBS and supports deregulation that aids the garbage producers of pop culture in the name of free enterprise. The left, while generally supporting the regulation of big business, claim that all "cultures" are equally valid and eschew censorship and control of cultural products. Both the political correctness of the left and the patriotic correctness of the right are combining to devastating effect.

While most corporate-media leaders still support the FCC, at least in principle, they do so only insofar as the regulatory agency's main role has come to be protecting the industry from internal poaching on assigned frequencies. In other words, the FCC clearly protects the industry more than it does the public. What is more, political action by companies in the telecommunications business is rabidly intense. Media lobbyists work the corridors of Washington, speaking with influence that other lobbyists could only hope to have, since politicians fear what the media can do to their public images (Bagdikian).

Interestingly, the work of these lobbyists is not limited to American-held corporations. Writing for *Communication Research* in 1992, Joseph Turow explained the new media mergers in terms of a general trend for "the globalization of mass media activities" combined with age-old greed on the part of business leaders for more profits (687). Among the largest players in today's global media game are Japan-based Sony Corporation and Rupert Murdoch's Australian holding company, News Corporation. Murdoch (the Fox Network, Fox Cable), who had been pressing for more FCC deregulation, was a big winner when Congress, as expected, passed the Telecommunications Act, eliminating most of the rules that restricted a company from owning more than twelve television stations. Working with his lobbyist, Peggy Binzel, Murdoch had organized a coalition with the three networks and the Tribune Company that successfully persuaded the Senate to eliminate the numerical limits on ownership, and he has been quoted as saying, "Deregulation is in the public interest" (see Edmund L. Andrews' "Mr. Murdoch Goes to Washington: The G.O.P. Welcome Is Warm Indeed," *The New York Times* July 23, 1995). We seriously doubt that, but one thing is certain: it's in Murdoch's interest. He also actively fended off efforts by the FCC to enforce foreign-ownership limits on his company. In the past, he was able to use the old rules to buy 20% to 25% ownership in stations all over the United States, and those stations currently reach roughly 35% of the nation's population.

The FCC recently ruled that it would not be in the "public interest" to divest Murdoch of his stations, even though he had violated the foreign-ownership limits, which prohibit holdings of more than 25% of any station. Although Murdoch became a U.S. citizen to get around this rule, the FCC is well aware that his holding company is located in Adelaide, Australia. Their ruling favoring one entrepreneur over the public interest is matched in audacity only by the fact that Murdoch also made a $4.5 million book deal with House Speaker Newt Gingrich.

Finally, Murdoch also supported the elimination of rules that prohibited companies from owning a newspaper and a television station in the same market and television stations in competing markets. Regarding the latter, on August 24, 1995, the FCC ruled again in Murdoch's favor by allowing him to own TV stations in the overlapping New York (largest) and Philadelphia (fourth largest) markets. Echoing both Murdoch himself and its own earlier ruling in his favor, the FCC deemed its action "in the public interest." Edmund L. Andrews hits the bull's eye when he titles one of his *New York Times* pieces on Murdoch, "Ownership Limits a Problem? Just Change the Rules." That's precisely what Murdoch and his cohorts did. In fact, according to John Malone, the CEO of cable giant Tele-Communications, Inc., it was Murdoch himself "who has established the norm for the worldwide, vertically integrated strategy." Now, Malone concludes, the other companies must try to catch up (see Kevin Maney's "Media Firms Shift to Gain Product Control," *USA Today*, September 14, 1995).

Some Republicans in Congress and some corporate leaders are currently calling for the complete elimination of the FCC over the next three years. The first step in this direction involved the elimination of the old fin-syn rules, which had effectively prohibited networks from having financial interests in the programs they aired or from profiting on the rerunning of these programs in syndication and which were allowed to expire, as predicted, on November 1, 1995. According to the June 5, 1995, issue of *Broadcasting and Cable*, the industry's trade publication, one of the groups calling for elimination of the FCC is the Progress and Freedom Foundation, which not so incidentally provided 80% of the funding for House Speaker Newt Gingrich's college courses carried on National Empowerment Television. Even if such complete deregulation should occur eventually, the industry would have little to fear since individual companies would then rely on the courts to protect their business rights in signal interference and other matters. Antitrust actions are likely to remain as quiescent as they are at the moment, even by a government that sees fit to attempt legislative regulation of "family values" and morality in popular art. (Ironically, these same voices would leave it to the family to regulate the toxic-waste sites of talk television.)

And there are other possible reasons for this cozy relationship between government and industry, as suggested in Bagdikian's *Media Monopoly*: "Consolidated control over the mass media has congealed at a tenuous time in national history. . . . Politicians do not often take issue with a corporation that controls their public image. It is unlikely that any administration in the foreseeable future will use antitrust law to reduce holdings of dominant media corporations" (224). Fear and pressure are not the only weapons that the media giants have in their arsenals—they also have money and a lot of it. According to the Center for Responsive Government, the communications industry contributed nearly $10 million directly to political action committees. Such "friendly persuasion" of the very policymakers we've elected to represent our interests cannot help but pay large dividends to the corporate elite.

Again, what is good for big business and for individuals in government may be disastrous for the rest of us. The real danger to the public of a weakened regulatory agency and lax rules about corporate media holdings comes from the diminishing number of voices heard on the airwaves, despite the multiplicity of channels and, therefore, the illusion of more choice. Recent changes in rules, even before passage of the Telecommunications Act of 1996, have allowed for cross-ownership of radio and television stations by media conglomerates (notably Time Warner, Sony, Viacom, Turner, Tribune, and, most recently, Westinghouse/CBS (television) and Westinghouse Infinity (radio). This policy severely threatens diversity of opinion and corporate accountability. Small independent operators have little chance against media giants, and with constricted government support, public-television stations will either have to become commercialized themselves or decline in their ability to purchase and/or produce quality programming. In the name of free enterprise, a handful of movers and shakers can claim that they have won the competition fair and square and that, besides, they're merely giving the American public what it wants anyway. (While we are watching these mind-numbing talk shows, they are buying up the media. In fact, one might even be forgiven for paranoid thoughts about a "plot" to keep us dumb.)

What is not in their interest to publicize is the vastness of their revenues and their holdings, which include radio, TV, programming, syndication, and print. Almost all of the talk shows considered in this book are syndicated by huge conglomerates: Sony (Ricki Lake), Tribune (Geraldo Rivera), Viacom (Maury Povich and Montel Williams), Time Warner (Jenny Jones), Multimedia (Phil Donahue, Sally Jessy Raphael, and Jerry Springer), Chris-Craft (Richard Bey), and King World (Oprah Winfrey, Rolonda Watts, and, most recently, a share in Geraldo Rivera). The only exception is Gordon Elliott's CBS network program. However,

CBS, the only remaining independent network of the original big three, in the summer of 1985 agreed to merge with Westinghouse Electric. In November 1995 the FCC gave its final approval to Westinghouse's $5.4 billion takeover of CBS; a merger that creates the nation's largest broadcaster (Aversa, "Final").

Increasingly, ratings and revenues will drive program content and format as the few media titans compete for the mass audience. One of the ways to get that audience is to air extreme talk, which, from the safe remove that TV provides, people find very entertaining and which producers find most lucrative. The main reason that toxic-talk shows are attractive to the corporate bottom-liners is that they are cheap to produce, requiring little in the way of actors, script writers, sets, and other expensive production items. Thus, they return much higher net profits to these media companies than the fictional TV programs they produce and distribute, like soap operas and prime-time shows. In *How to Watch TV News*, Neil Postman and Steve Powers estimate that the average entertainment hour costs $900,000 to produce, while the average news show comes in at about $500,000. The talk shows are even cheaper. Heaton and Wilson in *Tuning in Trouble* estimate that the average talk show costs one tenth of that—about $50,000 a segment or about $10 million to $20 million a year (32). Postman and Powers draw the only message one can draw from these staggering differences in corporate outlay: "More viewers, higher ratings, more advertising dollars, more profit, more similar programs to try to attract more viewers . . . ad infinitum" (6). Combine the profit potential with the staggering costs involved in these vast media acquisitions and the claim that the American public supposedly "wants" this product, and it becomes easy to conclude that this kind of toxic programming will continue to infect an already weakened social organism.

Even as we write, transforming concentrations of media ownership, most notably television, have put this issue into the daily headlines and made 1995 the watershed year for acquisitions and rumored takeovers, invited and hostile, while 1996 became the watershed year for enabling legislation in the form of the sweepingly deregulating Telecommunications Act. In *Networks of Power*, Mazzocco accurately writes that the "corporate engines that run the U.S. economy rely on uninterrupted transmission of their marketing and ideological images and messages to a national audience" (x). What with the massive debt being incurred by these conglomerates, accordingly, television will clearly have to pay even more attention now to that bottom line, and corporate bean counters will need to combine with pandering producers willing to satisfy any and all demands by voracious audiences and even to create more demand for their wares. Along with the editors of *The New York Times* whose September 2, 1995, editorial we cite earlier in this chapter, we worry that "with audiences guaranteed, we will get the lowest common-denominator junk—more Geraldo clones on the tube" (18). To be sure, this is good news for the talk shows, which will no doubt reach deeper for cheap thrills. And, for our part, most of us will likely ignore, as we do now, the complex relationships that the media have with corporate power structures.

However contaminating the current talk shows are, though, such "toxic talk" is only a small portion of the social consequences taking shape because of the media conglomerations. As cross-media ownership of newspapers, magazines, television, and radio intensifies, the most likely result will be a cookie-cutter approach to dispensing information, again providing the public with the illusion of many choices but in actuality projecting relatively few voices. As Frank Rich said in a recent *New York Times* opinion piece, "The fewer corporate giants who control the content of what we see, hear, and read, the fewer choices—no matter how large the increase in outlets for their cultural products. . . . In a corporate culture, original and idiosyncratic artistic voices, which by definition reach smaller markets, have trouble making themselves heard. . . . As our entertainment behemoths become larger, these essential alternative voices will have to fight harder to keep from being drowned out entirely" (A19).

Among the most troubling of these increasingly drowned-out voices is that of print journalism. As the corporate relationships between print and electronic media are cemented, the differences between them in terms of how and what they communicate, their style and content, will diminish. Daily newspapers have traditionally not catered to the same audiences as those of television and radio, and they have enjoyed special privileges as a result of their taking the "high road." While the government has long regulated the broadcast media through licenses, newspapers were left more or less unfettered since they acted as free voices in a democratic society. As electronic and print media fall into the same corporate hands, however, can the special preserve of print possibly last?

The recent acquisition of Multimedia, one of the nation's top TV producers and syndicators, by Gannett, the largest newspaper company in America, provides a good case in point. As industry analyst John Morton aptly put the matter to *The Washington Post*, Multimedia, whose credits include the talk shows starring Phil Donahue, Sally Jessy Raphael, and Jerry Springer, "has a sure sense of the nation's bad taste" (quoted in Glaberson's "The Press: Bought and Sold and Gray All Over," *The New York Times*, July 30, 1995). While Multimedia is hardly alone in servicing such bad taste, Gannett will have to follow suit if they are to recover the $1.7 billion they paid to acquire the broadcast giant. (Of course, Gannett already has some practice with its popular but innocuous *USA Today*.) How long, we wonder, will it take before Gannett's newspapers and Multimedia's TV programs are fully integrated in subject, style, and tone centered around the lowest common denominator and focusing sharply on the bottom line? To be sure, this is not the style and image that the American press should aspire to, but with fewer and fewer independent newspapers in the nation's cities, it is the one that the corporate moneymakers will likely encourage.

Indeed, this blurring of the information/entertainment line is already happening in the electronic counterpart to printed news. With good cause, TV journalists and newscasters are worried about what is going to happen to public-affairs coverage as the conglomerates move in. In a July 31, 1995, *Good Morning, America* interview on the Disney/ABC merger, Charles Gibson spoke with Disney chief Michael Eisner and Capital Cities president Tom Murphy about the impact of these mergers on high-quality journalism at ABC. Mr. Murphy answered with his own question, asking Gibson whether he wasn't proud to be part of the Disney family. That's it! The probable result of these new "family ties" will be corporate decisions to make news more like infotainment, as evidenced by Diane Sawyer's *Prime Time Live* interview with Michael Jackson just in time for him to promote his new album and video. As Bill Kovich points out in an August 3, 1995, *New*

York Times opinion piece, "ABC's news division will now have to compete with the enormous energy of Disney's entertainment productions in a company in which ABC's value as an outlet for entertainment is paramount" (A25).

To be sure, entire books could and should be written on the subject of the new media conglomerates, and their far-reaching implications for citizens in a democracy. How can Adam Smith's reliance on "enlightened self-interest" in regulating the marketplace be maintained if it's the media's interests that frame our knowledge of our own? What follows is just a sampling of the interlocking business interests driven by these corporate titans.[4]

Time Warner

The syndicator of Jenny Jones's talk show, New York-based Time Warner was formed in 1989 when Time, Inc., paid $14.1 billion to merge with Warner Communications, Inc. It is the largest media and entertainment company in the world and the world's number-one copyright owner, creator, and distributor.

The company's publishing operations include some thirty titles, many of them among the most recognizable in the nation—*Time, Fortune, People, Sports Illustrated.* Its music empire is also the world's largest, with Warner/Chappell Publishers and forty record labels, including Warner Bros., Elektra, and Atlantic. The company owns a 63.27% interest in Time Warner Entertainment, which has been the number-one prime-time television production company for seven straight years. As a movie producer, it is responsible for the hit film *The Bridges of Madison County.* The owner of the popular HBO cable network, which includes Cinemax, Time Warner is the second largest cable-TV operator in the United States after Tele-Communications, Inc., and the owner of the Six Flags Theme Parks. Its interests even extend to other media companies, including Turner Broadcasting of which Time Warner owns a 19.4% share. Its 1994 revenues of some $16 billion were surpassed only by Disney's, though it is also heavily in debt owing to recent acquisitions (see Turner Broadcasting System below).

Nevertheless, on August 29, 1995, Time Warner announced that it was ready to make an $8.5 billion offer to acquire the Turner Broadcasting System, a deal that would make the resulting media company the largest in the world, with annual revenues of more than $19 billion, surpassing both Disney/ABC and Westinghouse/CBS. Before he would approve the deal, however, powerful Turner board member John Malone of Tele-Communications, Inc., the cable giant, had to be satisfied, notably about how his 21% stake in Turner would be converted into Time Warner stock (Wollenberg C1). During the same week that Time Warner broke this news, General Electric, which had long been interested in acquiring Turner, announced plans for either a counteroffer to Turner or the acquisition of Time Warner itself. In a *Philadelphia Inquirer* article discussing the Time Warner/Turner deal among others, *Los Angeles Times* columnist Martha Groves again answers the question "What's behind this summer's [1995] feeding frenzy? . . . The activity was set off by Disney's $19 billion play for Capital Cities/ABC. The big fish devouring their smaller counterparts are taking advantage of an unusual convergence of forces—a friendly political and regulatory atmosphere in Washington, the growing global appetite for entertainment, the long bull market on Wall Street and the coming of age of sophisticated technologies that make it possible to distribute content worldwide in new, less expensive ways. The shifts are dramatic. . . . [They] pave the way for an industry of vertically integrated powerhouses with extensive control over both the content and distribution of programming" (C3).

Viacom

The world's number-two media giant after Time Warner, New York-based Viacom, was formed by CBS in 1970 when the FCC's fin-syn rulings against financial interest in programming that networks carried also prohibited television networks from owning cable systems and TV stations in the same markets. Viacom took over CBS's program syndication division and subsequently bought cable systems in five states. It formed the Showtime subscription service in 1978 and became a full owner in 1982.

Viacom did not enter the modern media age, however, until it was purchased in 1987 for $3.4 billion by its current chairman, Sumner Redstone, through his movie theater chain, National Amusements. Redstone, who owns about half of the company's common stock, scored a coup in 1994 when he won a bidding war for Paramount Pictures and later for Blockbuster Video, the world's top video and music retailer. In early 1995, Viacom, along with New York–based Chris-Craft, launched United Paramount Network, a fifth major TV network, which is expected to reach 47% of the nation. With respect to television, it distributes Maury Povich's talk show and is one of several involved in the distribution of Montel Williams's program; it is also a syndicator of the *Star Trek* series, *Cheers*, and *Taxi*. Viacom also owns such basic-cable channels as MTV, VH-1, and Nickelodeon, and premium stations as Showtime and The Movie Channel, and it has a 50% share of the USA Network, Comedy Central, the Sci-Fi Channel, and the All-News Channel. As a producer of leading television programs, Viacom is responsible for *Frazier*, *Entertainment Tonight*, *Melrose Place*, and *Beverly Hills 90210*. In addition to television, its movie studio, Paramount Pictures, is expected to turn a handsome profit on hits like Academy Award winner *Forrest Gump*, which is expected to bring Viacom more than $200 million in sales.

In addition, Viacom owns several major book publishers, including Simon & Schuster, Macmillan USA, Scribner, Prentice Hall, and Pocket Books, along with scores of radio and TV stations and movie theaters throughout the U.S., Canada, and Europe. Finally, its holdings include Paramount's five theme parks in the United States and Canada, the Discovery Zone, and various interactive-media companies. Viacom's 1994 sales topped $7.3 billion.

On July 25, 1995, it announced plans to spin-off its cable system, Tele-Communications, Inc. The approximately $2 billion deal was approved on a tax-free basis by the IRS in June 1996 (Landler D1).

Turner Broadcasting System

With 1994 revenues of $2.8 billion, the Atlanta-based originator of CNN is the creation of the brash and ambitious Ted Turner. The company's holdings are wide ranging, indeed, from programming (TBS, TNT, and the Cartoon Network) to production and distribution (New Line Cinema, Castle Rock Entertainment, and Hanna-Barbera Cartoons) to news (CNN Headline News, and CNN International). Other holdings include the Atlanta Braves baseball team and World Championship Wrestling.

Despite his enormous financial success, Ted Turner's greatest ambition has been to own a network (Wollenberg, "Time"). He made a failed bid for CBS in the eighties, and now, on the heels of Westinghouse's $5.4 billion offer to acquire CBS in 1995, he tried to acquire the funding necessary to make a $6 billion counteroffer. Without board approval, however, he could not spend more than $2 million. The largest stockholders on that board were also media giants—Time Warner and Tele-Communications, Inc., the nation's largest cable-TV system. Until now, Time Warner had opposed Turner's network ambitions, but it has had a change of heart for its own reasons. More than $15 billion in debt, Time Warner believed that the acquisition of CBS would raise the value of its Turner stock, which could be sold off later to help finance its own debts. (For his part, Turner turned down Time Warner's offer to sell its holdings for $1.6 billion in cash or a Turner asset like the Cartoon Network.) Hoping to raise the necessary cash to buy CBS or to buy out Time Warner's stake in TBS, Turner considered purchasing the cash-rich King World so that he could use their resources as assets. Turner's board rejected the idea. The board members with lion's share of the say, Time Warner and Tele-Communications, Inc., argued that their decision was based on the fact that King World's largest moneymaker, Oprah Winfrey, would have the right to leave the company if it was sold, and they didn't see any point to owning King World without her. Turner approached Bill Gates of the Microsoft Corporation to become a billion-dollar partner in his network plans. Gates considered the offer. Turner is also currently trying to buy the Samuel Goldwyn Company, whose holdings include movie theaters and a film library.

As noted above (see Time Warner), the newest wrinkle in Turner's fortunes was Time Warner's purchase of Turner Broadcasting for $8.5 billion, and GE's interest in acquiring Turner or the "new and improved" Time Warner itself. Turner was said to be extremely pleased with all of this interest in his company. As Michael Rozansky wrote in *The Philadelphia Inquirer*'s September 17, 1995, issue, "Turner reportedly had been looking at ways to buy out Time Warner's stake in his company. Now, instead of getting divorced, he's getting married, in a deal that [Time Warner Chairman] Levin apparently thinks will firmly establish his own imprint on the company" (D1). Rather ironically, to say the least,

Turner recently spoke out on C-SPAN (May 1996) against the merging of media corporations and implied that the ensuing monopolies were dangerous. *New York Times* columnist Frank Rich writes, "Ted Turner, speaking at Harvard Law School this month, said flatly that television 'exploits children' and 'has an overall negative effect on society.' Even the fact that he is selling his own TV empire to Time Warner did not prevent Mr. Turner from describing today's gargantuan media conglomerates, of which Time Warner is the second-largest, as 'frightening'" (A19). But we suppose that in the end, his fears are ameliorated greatly by the fun of acquisition and sale and the bottom line.

Disney

The company built by a mouse and a duck entered the modern media age when ex-Paramount studio chief Michael Eisner took the helm in 1984. The Disney Corporation's recent acquisition of Capital Cities/ABC, Inc. for $19.2 billion, the second-largest takeover in history, launches the venerable company into the media stratosphere as the world's largest media conglomerate with $16.5 billion in annual revenues (Fabrikant D1, D6).

It also becomes one of the nation's largest companies, with a market value of $40 billion and holdings that include the country's top-rated TV network, movie companies (Miramax, Hollywood Pictures, Touchstone, and, of course, Disney), the Disney film library, the four Disney theme parks worldwide, the Disney channel and ESPN on cable, ten local television stations and twenty-one radio stations, licensing and production of Disney merchandise, and 265 retail stores worldwide. Its recent feature films— *Aladdin*, *The Lion King*, and *Pocahontas*—are the most successful animated films in history, and it has now extended itself beyond its typical family entertainment with Hollywood Pictures' erotic thriller *The Color of Night*. Its successful TV series include *Home Improvement*, and the 1994 musical version of *Beauty and the Beast* represented Disney's debut on the Broadway stage.

For its part, Capital Cities/ABC owns ten television stations, reaching 25% of American homes, as well as *Women's Wear Daily* and seven newspapers, including *The Kansas City Star*. Through this merger, Disney became the first media company with a major presence in four markets: film, broadcasting, cable TV, and telephone lines through its joint ventures with several regional phone companies. Despite its solid positioning in the industry, rapid changes in broadcasting prompted the Disney Corporation to make its recent maneuvers. One of the reasons cited for the ABC deal was Disney's fear, given the expiration of the fin-syn rules, that it would have trouble selling its programs now that the broadcast networks are no longer bound by FCC regulations limiting the production of in-house television programming.

Ironically, ABC itself was born out of the regulatory spirit prevalent at the dawn of TV. In 1943, RCA owned two networks, the Red and the Blue. Fearing that RCA would monopolize the fledgling television industry, the FCC ordered RCA to give one up, and the Blue network was then sold to Ed Noble of Lifesavers Candy, who renamed it the American Broadcasting Company (ABC) (Auletta 30). The company, with the help of Disney, is now taking advantage of the deregulatory direction of things. With the networks allowed for the first time since fin-syn rules went into effect to broadcast programs that they also produce, Disney will be able to show its cartoons on network TV, a move that will seriously affect its programmer-producer competitors like Warner Brothers, a unit of Time Warner. As a result of Disney's new-found influence, producers like Time Warner are more cautious about buying stakes in networks, one of the reasons cited for originally opposing Ted Turner's bid for CBS. Time Warner's decision to purchase Turner Broadcasting for $8.5 billion obviously represents part of its competitive strategy to market its cartoons and other products. The Disney/ABC annual sales figures are expected in 1996 to top $16.5 billion, the largest in the industry by far. If the Time Warner/Turner deal goes through, however, the media conglomerate would surpass Disney, taking in some $19 billion annually.

As an interesting and ironic footnote, just days after the announcement of the Time Warner interest in acquiring Turner, a Virginia-based religious group, the American Life League, charged that Disney was subliminally planting sexually explicit messages and scenes in its animated family features (see Aly Sujo's "Va. Group Assails Disney's Character," *The Philadelphia Inquirer*, September 3, 1995: A3). The group claims that the word "SEX" appears in a dust cloud in *The Lion King*, that *Aladdin* has a subliminal message to teenagers to take off their clothes, and that *The Little Mermaid* shows a character in sexual arousal. Others in the film industry have added that *Who Framed Roger Rabbit?* has a single frame showing frontal nudity. While Disney denies the charges, saying that they are matters of perception, industry insiders say that the claims are true and speculate that these subliminal manipulations are either jokes or the work of subversive animators. One animated frame is even said to contain Michael Eisner's home telephone number.

Judie Brown, the president of the American Life League, has been quoted as saying, "I don't know what Michael Eisner thinks he's doing. I have no way of knowing what their plan is for our kids. But they're making a fortune, and these cartoons are filled with sexual imagery. A lot of young mothers are very, very upset" (Sujo A3). Despite Disney spokesman Rick Rhoades's dismissal of the allegations as "ridiculous," that parental "upset" comes at a bad time in Disney's plans for strategic media positioning.

Nevertheless, it strikes us as ironic that these right-wing forces raise such objections about real and perceived sexual content in Disney's programs while ignoring completely the implications of its role and potential financial windfalls in the shrinking media market.

Gannett/Multimedia

Under CEO John Curley, the newspaper goliath recently acquired Multimedia, one of the nation's top TV producers and syndicators, for $1.7 billion. Gannett is the largest newspaper company in America with annual revenues of $3.8 billion, and Multimedia's revenues for 1994 topped $630 million, which makes for a very profitable combined operation (Fabrikant D1, D6).

As of 1995, Multimedia owned six television stations, eleven dailies, and forty-nine other newspapers. It also operated 160 cable television franchises in Illinois, Kansas, North Carolina, and Oklahoma, serving 450,000 subscribers. In addition to its national newspaper, *USA Today*, Gannett owned 82 dailies with a circulation of more than six million. It also operated ten television stations and eleven radio stations and is the largest outdoor advertising company in North America.

Interestingly, one of those who profited the most from the deal and who might best help to bridge the gap between news and entertainment is none other than Phil Donahue himself. As a major stockholder in Multimedia, he made a windfall in the acquisition. More important, Donahue is an "equity participant," producer, and occasional guest host of Multimedia's fledgling cable network, NewsTalk Television, which currently reaches two million viewers and which is being cited as a video outlet for Gannett's largest circulation daily, *USA Today* (Wechsler and Friedman 11-12).

Westinghouse

With its $5.4 billion purchase of CBS, the last of the original television networks, the Pittsburgh-based Westinghouse Electric Corporation became the most diversified of the media giants. The company, which, under CEO Michael H. Jordan, showed a profit in 1994 for the first time since 1990, is organized around eight businesses: electronics systems for radar, space, and military applications; government and environmental services, including hazardous-waste disposal; power generation; energy systems, including nuclear fuel; mobile refrigeration (Thermo King); real estate (WCI Communities); office equipment (The Knoll Group); and, of course, broadcasting (Group W). Under Jordan's leadership since 1993, the company has sold off some businesses (e.g., Westinghouse Electric Supply Company) and acquired others, including United Technologies Corporation's $220 million radar unit, Norden Systems. It also expanded its nuclear and non-nuclear power operations to the Czech Republic, Asia, and Latin America.

The Group W broadcasting group, which owns TV and radio stations and cable-TV systems, produced record sales and profits in 1994, thanks to a joint venture with CBS that increased its holdings from five to eight television stations. The CBS acquisition brought the total holdings to 15 television stations, 39 AM and FM radio stations, and production and syndication operations, not to mention CBS's earning power, which, in 1994, topped $3 billion. The Westinghouse Corporation's total worldwide sales in 1994 topped $8.8 billion. Most recently Westinghouse announced the biggest merger in radio history when they agreed to buy number-two Infinity Broadcasting for $3.9 billion. It would result in the combined company's owning 79 stations in 17 markets. "While there are companies that own more stations . . . none comes close to generating as much revenue" (Carter A1). Reporting on this story, *The Philadelphia Inquirer* pointed out that the deal now made partners out of previously fierce competitors within the Philadelphia market. Additionally the broadcast rights to all local major pro teams would be owned by the new giant called CBS Radio-Infinity.

Newscorp

Australian Rupert Murdoch scored big with this Adelaide-based company. The prototypical media mogul with worldwide interests, Murdoch turned a publishing group into a mass-media empire which many media insiders predicted would fail. He acquired Twentieth Century Fox in 1985 and later bought up six TV stations in large cities from Multimedia for almost $2 billion in order to launch a fourth national network, the Fox Broadcasting Company. Of course, the studio would allow him to produce shows that he could then broadcast on his network—something comparable to what Disney hoped to accomplish with the ABC acquisition (Sloan 25).

Murdoch also owns Asian and European satellite television networks, *TV Guide* Magazine, HarperCollins Publishing, and Delphi Internet Services. Most recently, he clashed publicly with Time Warner/Turner when he tried to get his Fox News Channel on Time Warner Cable in New York. When he lost his bid, he took revenge by refusing to give Ted Turner and his wife, Jane Fonda, the requisite number of adoring close-ups during Fox's broadcast of the 1996 World Series (see Rich, November 13, 1996: A23).

Sony

This Japanese electronics giant first invaded Hollywood when it purchased Columbia Pictures for $4.8 billion in 1989, but it really did not enter the big-time entertainment business until the early 1990s. A recent book about the deal, *Hit & Run: How Jon Peters and Peter Guber Took Sony for a Ride in Hollywood*, indicates that Sony's trust in the wrong people ended up costing Sony some $3 billion in losses. Nevertheless it is hard to worry about Sony's general future in the American entertainment market. Originally, Sony's reason for entering this market was so that it could promote its original business—hardware in the form of tape and CD players, TVs and VCRs—but it found the record, movie, and tape business too lucrative to be second best. In fact, 1994 U.S. entertainment sales alone accounted for $11.2 billion of the company's $36 billion take that year, and its entertainment investments are now equal to those of its electronics outlays in Japan. CEO Norio Ohga believes that the U.S. market for both entertainment and electronics will continue to bring large returns, even outpacing those of other markets, and the two divisions were consolidated in 1993 under the leadership of CEO Michael Schulhof.

Its entertainment assets, housed under Sony Music Entertainment and Sony Pictures Entertainment, include Columbia and Tri-Star film studios, Loews cinemas, and Columbia and Epic Records, and its electronics empire markets all manner of consumer products, including the enormously popular Walkman and Discman. Sony also holds a top slot in the talk-show arena, owning Ricki Lake's program as well as the failed talk show hosted by *Cosby* star Tempestt Bledsoe, both of which were regularly promoted on Sony OnLine, the company's Internet page.

Tribune

A leading entertainment and information company, the Chicago-based Tribune Company owns *The Chicago Tribune*, WGN-TV in Chicago, KTLA-TV in Los Angeles, the Chicago Cubs baseball team, an 8% share of America Online, and, of course, Geraldo Rivera's talk show, in association with his own Investigative News Group. In addition to producing newsprint and chemical byproducts, the Tribune owns six daily newspapers, seven independent television stations, and six radio stations.

Executive VP for Broadcasting Jim Dowdle would like to tie in newspapers and broadcast and cable TV in a three-way venture. "We're in communication with people in various markets who could be partners," he told *Broadcasting and Cable* (March 22, 1993). "We have the Orlando newspaper, the Fort Lauderdale newspaper, and the idea of the newspapers getting together with a cable and broadcast outlet there is conceivable" (15-17). His own hometown cable creation, ChicagoLand, is an around-the-clock news network, and he has also reshaped the company's flagship station, WGN-TV, into a major national cable service. *Broadcasting and Cable* estimated that WGN's revenues in 1992 were about $150 million, $15 million to $20 million of which came from national service.

In 1993 and 1994, Tribune moved into the reference publishing, interactive media, and educational software business. Formed in 1994 as part of a corporate restructuring, its Tribune New Media/Education division acquired for about $200 million Contemporary Books, Compton's Publishing, CD-ROM publisher Compton's NewMedia, and the Wright Group. Compton's, the oldest of Tribune's acquisitions, was founded in 1922 and purchased by Encyclopedia Britannica in 1961. Contemporary Books, a publisher of nonfiction and adult education books, was founded in 1946 as the Henry Regnery Company. When Tribune acquired the company, it was the second largest publisher of adult-education books in the U.S. The New Media/Education division will have as its primary focus the expansion of Tribune's multimedia publishing business as well as the development of technological links with its broadcasting and on-line holdings. This division added about $10 million to Tribune's bottom line in 1994.

King World

This New York company is the leading syndicator of TV programs in the United States, and its credits include a number of top-rated programs, including *Wheel of Fortune*, the world's most watched program, *Jeopardy*, the second most popular syndicated program since 1985, and *Inside Edition*, the world's most popular general-interest newsmagazine. In the talk-show arena, it is the syndicator of *Oprah*, the most successful talk show in TV history, and *Rolonda*. Its program library includes 210 television programs, sixty-eight feature films, and a number of film series, including The Little Rascals, Sherlock Holmes, Charlie Chan, and the East Side Kids. King World also distributes TV programs and feature-length films to about 400 stations in the U.S. and licenses programs in many foreign countries. It is also part owner of a TV station in Buffalo and of the interactive game manufacturer, Crystal Dynamics.

Although cash rich and debt free (the reason that Ted Turner considered buying the company so that he could finance his bid for CBS), King World's future as a leading syndicator of game, talk, and tabloid shows is in some doubt owing to the FCC decision to strike down the twenty-five-year-old "prime-time access rule." Part of the old fin-syn regulations, this rule prohibited networks from supplying programs for the 7 to 8 P.M. slot and was unintentionally responsible for the creation of large syndicators like King World, which supplied "appropriate" entertainment for that time slot. As we have already suggested, what started out as a noble government effort to limit the broadcast power of the networks and to allow for more diverse programming turned into a mega-industry and, in the process, further cheapened the level of American television. Striking the rule down by a vote of 5-0, the FCC allowed networks to enter the syndication business on August 30, 1996. Commission chairman Reed Hundt said the decision "simply reflected the commission's commitment to deregulation and free-market competition."

Other Megadealers

In June 1995, Seagram's chief Edgar Bronfman, Jr., who also owns a piece of Time Warner, paid the Matsushita Electric Industrial Corporation $5.7 billion for 80% of entertainment giant MCA. MCA owns Universal Studios, MCA Records, Geffen Records, and more than 40% of the Cineplex Odeon Corporation.

Steven Spielberg, David Geffen, and Jeffrey Katzenberg's studio, DreamWorks SKG, is negotiating with Bill Gates of Microsoft a deal that would bring interactive TV closer to reality.

In his 1991 book, *Three Blind Mice*, Ken Auletta argued that what has been occurring is the struggle for supremacy by five sovereign powers—the networks, cable TV, the independent and affiliated stations, the Hollywood studios, and the telephone companies. The outcome of this struggle, Auletta continues, is dependent on a sixth titan, Washington. "No one can know which of these sovereign powers will join forces to shape the vertically integrated communications colossus of the future, if indeed there is a future" (576). Since Auletta's book appeared, the contours of that colossus have become somewhat clearer, and, unfortunately, it includes more than five sovereign powers, each in a single business. Rather, it is a monster with many heads, including print journalism (Gannett), entertainment hardware (Sony), and even government, military, and industrial products and contracting (Westinghouse and General Electric).

The handful of players in these high-stakes games call their activities "synergy." But as Benjamin R. Barber points out in his book *Jihad vs. McWorld*, "synergy turns out to be a polite way of saying monopoly. And in the domain of information, monopoly is a polite word for uniformity" (137). *Newsweek*, whose August 14, 1995, story on Disney's acquisition of Capital Cities/ABC quotes Barber, uses the current and more euphemistic term "vertical integration" to describe the practices of those who built the railroads and other industries in the nineteenth century and the communications industry in our time (21).

Like their earlier historical counterparts, too, the contemporary media moguls have also invested considerable ego and ambition in their struggle to be the biggest and the most lucrative of the communications corporations. Commenting on the Turner/Time Warner deal, Turner biographer and *Wall Street Journal* television critic Robert Goldberg has said, "The thing that drives this deal and the thing that endangers it, paradoxically, are the egos and aspirations of the people at the top." And in a broader assessment, James M. Meyer, research director at Janny Montgomery Scott, has asserted, "It's empire building. . . . There are people out there like Michael Eisner and Ted Turner and Barry Diller and Gerry Levin and Sumner Redstone who are fighting with each other to be the kingpin of entertainment" (qtd. in Michael Rozansky's "Turner and Time: A Deal or a Coup?" *The Philadelphia Inquirer*, September 17, 1995). In other words, it's a game with a great big playing board and a frighteningly small number of potential winners. However you look at it, this game is not in the best interests of the American people.

New technologies like fiber optics and digital compression will soon make available hundreds of channels, some of them interactive, and most of the networks may come to be controlled by a single corporate entity—the phone company. In yet another announced buyout even more mind-boggling than the ones already described, the Bell Atlantic Corporation and the Nynex Corporation will "merge." *The New York Times* reports the proposed deal is worth $20.8 billion (Landler D4). As competition shrinks through single-company control of the technology and, therefore, the programming, we may well witness the most unassailable monopoly in American history. Although the future of this vast network was considered in Congress, a good portion of the American public remains unaware of these developments, in part because it is not in the monopolistic interests of the major media to inform the general public and encourage their participation. The other reason may be even more frightening, namely, that many Americans may not care to follow the complicated trails of the media movers and shakers because they are too busy being diverted and entertained by those very parties who stand to gain the most. We may indeed be amusing ourselves—and our cultural way of life—to death.

The next chapter offers some suggestions for reconstructing the frames broken by the television producers and the megadealers and reestablishing the public interest as a more realistic rationale for broadcasting.

Notes

1. In many front-page articles and in-depth analyses, both *The New York Times* and *The Philadelphia Inquirer,* two well-respected papers, relied upon for much of our discussion of the media buy-out frenzy of 1995-1996, told the reading public of the complexity of these pending deals. Interestingly, despite frequent suggestions that the press is becoming more like sound-bite, celebrity-driven television to survive (e.g., "The Tabloidization of Culture," in James Fallows, *Breaking the News: How the Media Undermines American Democracy* [New York: Pantheon, 1996] and Howard Kurtz, *Media Circus: The Trouble with America's Newspapers* [New York: Times Books, 1993]), we found, with the exception of a handful of articles on Murdoch and Turner, almost a complete absence of any material about the personal lives or values and interests of the men who now control most of the media conglomerates. Newspapers focused, instead, on the acquisitions and the revenues involved. Perhaps that fact helps explain the public's quiet about this transformation in media ownership. There have been few, if any, outcries for antitrust action. Perhaps the public is just not interested in "straight news" after some fifty years of television news and ten years of television talk shows!

2. We depended upon Ken Aulettta's *Three Blind Mice* (New York: Random House, 1991, 31-38), and Erik Barnouw's *The Sponsor* (New York: Oxford University Press, 1978, 19-36) for much of this discussion of the commercial evolution of radio and television in the early days.

3. President Clinton's FCC Chairman, Reed Hundt, has largely confined himself to getting the television broadcasters to dedicate three hours a week for children's programming rather than trying to stem the rising tide of vertical monopolies. Ervin Duggan, president of PBS, raises the troubling question as to what the standards for deciding what "educational" shall be. He writes in a *New York Times* Op-Ed piece that PBS has worked with educators to create such programs in a noncommercial framework (A21). He is obviously dubious about what the commercial broadcasters will decide fulfills the criteria for a "children's program."

4. Sources for the information on the talk-show conglomerates include *Standard & Poor's 1995 Register, Standard & Poor's 500 Guide, 1996 Edition* (New York: McGraw Hill), and America Online's *Hoover's Handbook Database* (Austin: Reference Press, 1994, 1995).

7

Reconstructing the Frame: Beyond the Politics of Deceptive Talk

But when complaints are freely heard, deeply considered, and speedily reformed, then is the utmost bound of civil liberty obtained that wise men look for.

—John Milton,
"Areopagitica" (1644)

If we think [the people] not enlightened enough to exercise their control with wholesome discretion, the remedy is not to take it from them, but to inform their discretion.

—Thomas Jefferson,
letter to William Jarvis (1820)

We have lost our knowledge of how physically to connect things in our everyday world, except by car, telephone and TV. You might say the overall consequence is that we have lost our sense of consequence. . . . Likewise, there is a connection between disregard for the public realm—for public life in general—and the breakdown of public safety.

—James Howard Kunstler,
The Geography of Nowhere (1993)

The soft hegemony of American pop culture is . . . everywhere visible. . . . They are but pieces of a mesmerizing mediology that suffuses consciousness everywhere.

—Benjamin Barber,
Jihad vs. McWorld (1995)

Scenario: The topic of the day is "Getting Even with Abusive Relatives." It's been done before. They've all been done before, dozens of times over, around the clock and around the dial, but

153

that doesn't matter. If it works—that is to say, if it hypes up the studio audience, is provocative enough to get the millions at home to tune in, and sells advertising time to sponsors—choose it, use it, reuse it, abuse it. This is, after all, television, a televised game, but unlike street games and board games and sports, everybody wins in this game—the hosts and producers, the equity owners, the audiences, the sponsors. Surely there can't be any harm done when everybody wins, right?

The hostess attempts to greet her guests with her usual seeming warmth and concern, a winning performance that she's used for five years as her ratings and income soared and her worldwide audience grew to fifteen million. But today she looks somehow different. She eyes them suspiciously, speaks the introductions in short, clipped phrases, almost mocking them with her tone and facial expression. The director grows concerned but lets her go on. Assembled on stage together, the five guests, who are ready to enjoy their brush with fame, stare self-consciously into the camera as she introduces them.

There's Rashanda and her mother, Laverne. Rashanda, 23, is the unemployed mother of five children, all of them by different men with whom she currently has no contact, much less child-support payments. Currently expecting her sixth child, Rashanda is on welfare and lives with her mother, who used to work days as a waitress in a diner and evenings as a cleaning woman. Rashanda claims that her mother has badgered her for years, first to finish high school, then to get a job, then to stop getting pregnant or have her tubes tied, and now to give her kids up for adoption since the women can't support them any longer. Finally fed up with her mother's intrusive suggestions, Rashanda locked Laverne, 39, in a closet for three days so that, as the younger woman puts it, she would feel as "trapped" as Rashanda has felt all of these years. The mother claims that the harrowing experience of spending seventy-two hours in the dark without food or water did teach her not to meddle in her daughter's affairs. It also cost the older woman her two jobs. Now both are on welfare as they await Rashanda's sixth child.

There's also Garth, 14, and his common-law stepfather, Jesse, 22. Garth's mother, Jeannie, 29, sits between them. The victim of physical and sexual abuse since Jesse moved in with Jeannie three years before, Garth decided this year that he'd had enough. Getting the idea from watching true-crime TV shows, he asked a friend to rig up a video camera so that he could videotape Jesse's handiwork. Armed with the tape, Garth later threatened to have Jesse arrested, and the abuse stopped, mostly because, as a convicted felon, Jesse couldn't afford another appearance in front of the judge. Jeannie says, "I'm just relieved the conflict between the two men in my life is over now and we can live like a normal family." Before going to the first commercial break, the hostess promises to return with clips from Garth's secret video, and the audience lets out anticipatory groans. They are reminded of the Rodney King Show and can't wait to see this installment of the world as stage. Alas, however, they were all to be disappointed. The hostess has another show planned for today.

After the break, the hostess walks up to the guests on stage, eyes each of them individually, and says quietly, "What are you doing? Do you know what you're doing here today? You've volunteered to come on this show to talk about matters that are private, that are shameful, that reveal serious dysfunctionality within the family. You've come to entertain us with your stories of sin, complete with you-are-there videotapes, and you feel no shame or guilt over telling about your lives. And the people sitting in this audience are delighted that you feel no shame. They do about their own private matters, but they don't want you to feel the same way or else they can't be entertained, they can't laugh or cluck self-righteous tongues or advise you, in a minute or so, how to put your lives back on track.

"Let's keep private matters private, shall we?" she says, speaking earnestly to the audience now and to the camera. "We've heard all of this gruesome stuff before, and we aren't better off as a culture for having heard it. In fact, it's killing us. It's raising the underclass to an art form. It's telling the world that this is what America has become, a land where cheap thrills can be had by listening to tawdry stories.

"Let's talk today instead about the recent merger between Disney and ABC. What will this new vertical integration do to the entertainment and information business? Does anyone know what their combined holdings are? What are the implications for the American public? For children's programming? Who is Reed

Hundt? How is this new combination and the others being pro-posed by other media giants related to government deregulation? Have you heard about the Time Warner/Turner deal? What is a vertical monopoly, does anyone know? No one? Has anyone read a newspaper or book lately? If it's only The National Enquirer, don't tell me. In fact, I can see from your faces that you're not going to tell me anything, and so I guess there's nothing left to talk about.

"Goodbye and good luck, America!"

Discussing his upcoming addition to the new round of talk shows slated to appear in the 1995-96 television season, former *Partridge Family* star, radio personality, and recovering drug abuser Danny Bonaduce said that he'd figured out the whole talk-show "scam." "Some of the talk shows forget that no matter how seriously they treat a guy who is sleeping with his Rottweiler, it is just a freak show," he told *People* magazine. "People like that will not be on my show. They should be in some sort of therapy." Despite this claim, in the first week of production, he was already doing one of the most overdone and tired topics in the talk-show repertoire—crossdressers. It seems, however, that Bonaduce hadn't figured out as much of the "scam" as he suggested since his show was cancelled after only one season. Nevertheless, he was right about the last part—one would have hoped that a person, including a guest or host of these kinds of shows, would have to cross some threshold of credibility before being aired to millions of people.

Contrary to Bonaduce's and the other newcomers' promises to be "different," it's more likely that any new batch of talk shows sharing the basic premise and assumptions of the old will not improve upon but be more toxic than the programs put on by their distant predecessors (Oprah and Donahue) and their contemporary competition (Ricki, Jenny, and Springer). The vertical monopolies are likely to continue to feature this form of entertainment because it will sell if it's shocking (i.e., indecent, culturally "pornographic" in its dismantling of our civil cultural "programming") enough and because, as noted earlier, it's very inexpensive to produce. When all is said and done, profit is their basic premise and value assumption.

So what is the solution? Is there an antidote to contaminating talk? And if there is such an antidote, can it be or should it be forcefully administered to our culture? Those feeding us the poison say that we ought to be free to take it, that it's, in fact, our First Amendment right to demand it and theirs to broadcast it. Of course, the same specious argument, wrapped in the shiny foil of the Constitution, is advanced to justify all entrepreneurial activity in one way or another. The same argument has been advanced with regard to legalizing drugs, prostitution, and gambling, and yet, our culture has resisted the argument and has either prohibited or severely regulated activities that could cause severe personal and social harm. In other words, we have chosen, albeit often in a "shotgun" manner, to regulate certain activities and industries in the best interests of society, even if it has meant protecting individuals from their own desires or the endless possibilities that the human consciousness can invent, in this case the technology that allows for both the mass broadcasting of what was previously "unspeakable" negative behavior on the part of most of the "guests" and the competition to control the profits from the programming on the part of the capitalists. Clearly the ultimate solution lies in a rethinking of our values in the light of this amazing medium, or to use McLuhan's subtitle, the extensions of man. We now have the ability to do things we could never do before, and the question of how to devise a system of values concerning whether we *should* do them for fame or fortune (old values) is really basic to our democracy's survival in this electronic and atomic age.

In his satiric fiction *Candide* (1759), Voltaire repeatedly used the mocking phrase "the best of all possible worlds" to suggest ironically that this one is far from the best world imaginable. Apart from the natural disasters to which we are all subject, there are the problems brought about by the baser side of human desire. That is why civil societies have always tried to devise rules to curb or control such potentially destructive tendencies as unregulated appetite, greed, fraud, and "vices" like gambling and prostitution. Just so, in the best of all possible worlds, toxic talk would not exist, or if it did, a civic-minded populace would reject it, voting with their feet, their purses, or their remote controls. It would be nice if the reconstructed frame we're suggesting would come about by a renewed social vision, informed by morality and concern for others and driven by altruism or at least enlightened self-interest. That would be nice, but it is, in the immediate future, highly improbable.

The only feasible plan, until we develop new cultural standards and values to control and deal with the consequences of these inventions of our age, must involve our government—a government that takes its responsibilities toward the citizens seriously, as was the case when broadcasting was starting out. If the government shrugs its shoulders over its responsibility, the powerful few will act to the detriment of the many. Since the inception of television, the FCC has been, to say the least, inconsistent in its approach to the medium. The FCC was created in 1934 to act as a regulatory agency to watch over the public airwaves and, therefore, the public interest, functioning in much the same way that other regulatory agencies do (e.g., the Federal Aviation Administration). But beginning during the Nixon administration and intensifying through the Reagan and Bush years, the FCC (again, like other regulatory agencies) has been weakened in the name of laissez-faire competition. While the justification for deregulation has been public demand and public interest, the underlying philosophy and the effect on the public interest have been far from democratic. *Caveat emptor*—let the buyer, or viewer in this case, beware—might be a better statement of the corporate and governmental philosophy. In fact, recent rhetoric stresses the "responsibility" of parents to regulate their children's television consumption rather than the responsibility of the television producers and regulators to put out a "safe" product. The only antidote offered involves the First Amendment with people grinding their political axes on both political wings—those who would gut the First Amendment by means of severe censorship and, on the other hand, those who say that the First Amendment guarantees their right not to be regulated.

Of late, the print media have focused public attention on the controversial "Indecency Clause" of the Telecommunications Act of 1996 that would ban pornography on the burgeoning Internet.[1] Despite this focus, however, the general intent of the new law, as evidenced by its broad loosening of restrictions against cross-ownership of the media, is sweepingly laissez-faire. The government has clearly come down on the side of big business, and the Telecommunications Act of 1996 seems designed to support the media buyouts and megadeals.

If we look back at the original intent of the Federal Communications Act of 1934, which created the FCC, or the 1949 Fairness Doctrine, we find that what was to be regulated were the public airwaves for corporate economic interests, not free speech. Indeed, because the potential manipulative power of the airwaves was so great, it was prudently deemed necessary to subordinate the free speech of broadcasters to the greater public interest. Since the potential and technology for such manipulation are even greater today than in 1949, given the explosive growth of the medium in this century and our movement toward and now into the information age, it is critical that the federal government once again take up the responsibility of safeguarding the public. In particular, we recommend the following:

Reinvigorate the FCC and Stop Deregulation

The right of the FCC to monitor the airwaves in the public interest should be returned to its full vigor. Mark Fowler, President Reagan's first FCC chairman, decided to reframe things in 1981, claiming that "the only issue is freedom" to speak, to watch, to buy and sell station licenses, and to let the marketplace determine format and content of television shows. This policy helped bring about the vertical media monopolies that we see taking shape now, corporate entities that show no public responsibility except to their own individual stockholders. Giant media companies are "stocking the shelves" with as many of their own channels as possible to crowd out real competition. Moreover, few new smaller companies offer real alternative programming. In an October 23, 1996, opinion piece for *The New York Times*, Andrew Ehrenberg, a British marketing professor, correctly observes that "competition doesn't consist of being different from your competitors, but of being the same" (A25). Hence, far from bringing about greater freedom of choice, media monopolies have limited the real choices that Americans have. President Clinton's FCC chairman, Reed Hundt, has said that "the public has a huge stake in the communications revolution, and private interests should not own 100% of the action." And yet, there is far less program diversity today than there was before the FCC began to deregulate broadcasting in the 1970s, and corporate profits are at an all-time high.

Surely the imbalance of power here is clear. We need to bring about the conditions necessary for true competition as well as the protection of minority rights against mass ratings generated by massive marketing. We must have an expert telecommunications agency with the power to license, tax, bring criminal charges for conspiracy to impede competition, and generally scrutinize the interests and holdings of large media corporations. Imagine the poor standards to which food and drugs would fall without the FDA or airline safety without the FAA or air quality without the EPA or legalized gambling without casino regulatory agencies. Imagine profit-greedy companies free to "do their own thing" in these industries. The possibilities are grist for Stephen King's mill. Unfortunately, it's easier to imagine the low level to which information and entertainment would fall without a strong FCC. It's easier to imagine because the effects are already happening.

The government must take up again its responsibility to ensure that no company or group be allowed to monopolize production and distribution of media products. Accordingly, the FCC, the Justice Department, the Department of Commerce, and Congress should stop the current deregulatory trend by prohibiting corporate cross-ownership of broadcast, cable and print companies, limiting subsidiaries and holding companies from controlling too many radio and television stations, and actively promoting competition and diversity in the entertainment/information industry.

Ann Bingaman, the Justice Department's assistant attorney general for antitrust matters, recently admitted that the American public may be growing uneasy about the frenzied pace of the media mergers. Although she is looking into the $19 billion Disney-Cap Cities/ABC deal and the $5.4 billion Westinghouse-CBS merger, she declined to say whether she shared the nation's unease (see Robyn Meredith's "Media Deals," USA Today, September 14, 1995). We certainly hope she does and that she uses the government's authority to curb this dangerous trend. The antitrust legislation already on the books should be used to decrease acquisitions and the concentration of media power in fewer and fewer hands.

Treat TV as a Public Utility

In his recent book (with Craig LeMay), *Abandoned in the Wasteland: Children, Television and the First Amendment*, former FCC chairman Newton Minow argues that since the airwaves are essentially public property, we should expect at least a modicum of public service in return for letting businesses make huge profits. However, while Minow and LeMay suggest merely that Congress require broadcasters to meet a specified standard of programming for children, we think that such a limitation is too narrow. After all, adults watch TV, too, and we should expect the same public-interest programming and a significant say in the control of a medium that plays such an important role in shaping and controlling society. In short, television should be regarded as nothing less than a public utility, not a private corporate domain.

If television is regulated like all other public utilities, government can apply public-interest laws to regulate licensing, commercial airtime, and standards for news and community programming by all of the controlling parties—commercial networks, syndicators, cable stations, Hollywood producers of shows, and the like. At the present the federal government has just about erased any standards at all. Conversely, since the industry still, at least theoretically, constitutes a public trust, it can also cancel the "rented" licenses of those whose programming is misleading or otherwise dangerous to the public. In general, the purpose of FCC oversight is public safety, just as the FAA's is to regulate flight patterns and aircraft safety and the FDA's to set standards for drug testing and foods.

In turn, the producers of toxic talk should be held responsible for mislabeling their fraudulent products as "entertainment" or "socially useful discussion" or, worst of all, "therapy." The 1996 Decency Act does not go far enough and is unclear and not specific enough to deal with such programming that isn't obviously sexually graphic or physically violent. Moreover, producers and their corporations should be cited for polluting the airwaves and for not adequately disclosing the toxic "side effects" of their dangerous practices on their guest-victims and society at large. (Quantifying the damages ought to be a matter of serious legal attention.) Perhaps if such threats were taken seriously enough, the broadcasters would even become responsible for policing themselves and their competitors.

Take Action Against Deceptive and Offensive Language

The free-speech concept has never applied to commercial television (or, for that matter, to commercials themselves). The potential dangers of corporate control of the airwaves have always been recognized, and so the First Amendment right of those controlling the transmission media has been subordinated to the audience's right to be protected from certain kinds of speech. Strict limitations have been placed on the network programs' language and visual content, particularly between the hours of 6 A.M. and 10 P.M. In other words, because of the nature and influence of their messages, broadcasters do not possess the right to *free* speech but rather to *licensed* speech. And, like other industries, if this one wants to make a profit on this protected speech, it must put out a "safe" product. What we have seen on the toxic-talk shows, however, tells us that the windfall profits now being garnered depend not on product safety but on consumable trash.

While the talk shows do not fit the conventional definition of pornography or obscenity, which entail graphic pictures or descriptions of sexual activity, they certainly fit the indecency standard. The courts have broadly defined *indecency* as "patently offensive language or material that depicts sexual or excretory activities or organs." Since a great deal of what is described or acted out on the talk shows involves "patently offensive" descriptions of sexuality, they should be charged with indecency. On those occasions when the line is crossed and the sexual descriptions become graphic, statutes against obscenity should be applied.

Still, it has been difficult for the FCC to regulate obscenity and indecency and not cross the line into censorship, which was prohibited by Section 326 of the Communications Act of 1934. Much of its original language was retained in the Communications Decency Act of 1996. On the one hand, there is the law. Title 18, Section 1464, of the Federal Criminal Code prohibits broadcasting "obscene, indecent or profane language," and the penalty for violation is up to $100,000 in fines, two years' imprisonment, or both. On the other hand, the FCC uses its own definition in its monitoring of broadcast television, defining "indecency" as language and material that describes, in terms "patently offensive" as measured by contemporary community standards for the broadcast medium, "sexual or excretory activities or organs." While not excluded from First Amendment protection, indecency so defined has been determined unsuitable for the broadcast media by the FCC. (Cable TV, print, and now the Internet are excluded from such prohibitions.)

Despite the opposite trend, the time has certainly come to put teeth in both the FCC's oversight function and the federal law prohibiting obscenity and indecency on the public airwaves. The definitions above are serviceable, and violation of these restrictions should result in the loss of the broadcaster's license and/or stiff fines to broadcasters and advertisers. Such actions are not unprecedented. For instance, radio and television personality Howard Stern's bad language on the air has resulted in fines in the millions of dollars. Costly sanctions like these should be imposed for all manner of offensive and deceptive language, including indecent descriptions of sexuality, lying to the public, spreading malicious rumors, "outing" people who choose to keep their private lives private, and false advertising.

The question of how an audience is harmed by its interpretation of programming is a thorny one, dating back to the national panic caused by the 1938 radio broadcast of Orson Welles's *The War of the Worlds*. The courts have effectively shied away from declaring broadcasters liable for messages that lead to individual or collective antisocial behavior. It's time to place blame squarely where it belongs. In cases where the effects of harmful practices can be demonstrated—in many cases there is no doubt about cause and effect—criminal charges and public class-action lawsuits should be instituted. In fact, we are already seeing a handful of disgruntled "guests" bringing suit against these programs for misleading them about the effects of making disclosures on national television. Yvonne Porter of San Jose, California, has sued *The Montel Williams Show* for featuring her on a program about old boyfriends. On the air she learned that her own sister was sleeping with Yvonne's boyfriend. Because she was misled and humiliated on national television, she sued and won an undisclosed settlement. In another case, soap-opera actor Brent Jasmer of *The Bold and the Beautiful* has settled a suit against Geraldo Rivera's syndicator, Tribune. Jasmer, who was adopted as a child, was reunited with his biological mother on the program even though, he contends, the producers assured him the meeting would not occur on the air. Most recently, a Michigan woman has filed suit against *The Sally Jessy Raphael Show*. The woman maintains that her picture was erroneously identified by a man who appeared on Raphael's show as that of a female prison inmate to whom he proposed.

If well-publicized criminal actions, civil suits, and class-actions were initiated for slander, libel, defamation, fraud, and damaging the reputation of the so-called guests, we would see an avalanche of such suits, and the financial consequences of these actions would be enough to eliminate or limit TV's toxic talk's attack on our cultural capital.

Raise Fees, Limit Licenses, Impose Taxes

In *The Revolt of the Elites and the Betrayal of Democracy*, Christopher Lasch noted that we "need to set limits on the imperialism of the market, which transforms every social good into a commodity. . . . Today it is the elites—those who control the international flow of money and information . . . manage the instruments of cultural production and thus set the terms of public debate—that have lost faith in the values, or what remains of them, in the West" (25-26). The frenzied competition for more of an audience share can be controlled by issuing only a limited number of licenses each year and charging much more for the license to broadcast. Just as potential casino companies bid for the limited licenses available to build their bases of operation, the media companies should bid for the right to broadcast, and in turn, the FCC should investigate the bidding companies, setting stringent fitness requirements, closely scrutinizing the product to be broadcast and then following up after granting the license. Based on these investigations, of course, the FCC should then also have the right to deny licenses and subsequently revoke them for failure to follow through on promises or otherwise abusing the public trust, along with imposing fines and/or heavy taxes for failure to regard the public welfare. As with gambling consortia in the private sector, moreover, an original licensing fee and annual fees, both of these fees substantial, should be imposed.

Another possibility might be the imposition of "sin" taxes, much as we do with alcohol, tobacco, and gambling. For example, the tax on lottery tickets is fifty cents on the dollar whereas normal consumer items are taxed at a much lower rate, 6% on average. In this way, we might reduce the public debt and even finance alternative broadcasting possibilities. Others have made essentially the same point.

Dennis Mazzocco argues in his book *Networks of Power* that, since commercial television is allowed to use the public airwaves to make millions of dollars in advertising revenues from sponsors, they should also bear the brunt of financing meaningful alternative media in the United States. In fact, annually since 1993, upon purchase or sale broadcasters do not need to pay a fee for the airwaves they exploit. "When one considers," he goes on, "that in addition to not being obligated to pay a significant portion of revenues back to the public, all media operators are also eligible to claim huge federal and state tax deductions on programming costs as well as the interest on the debt to buy even more media properties, one realizes that the U.S. media monopoly that we currently have is a heavily subsidized public trust. Indeed, 100 percent of its profits go toward expanding private corporate empires that presently are under no obligation to fully disclose their finances or worldwide operations" (158).

Lawrence Grossman, the former president of NBC News and PBS, makes this point even more forcefully in a *New York Times* opinion piece ("Cut the Public in on the Mega-Mergers," August 21, 1995): "The nation is entitled to a decent return on public property—the airwaves that it gave away free to communications companies. The epidemic of media mega-mergers demonstrates the extraordinary financial value of the television and radio station licenses, cable franchises and cellular phone frequencies. . . . Telecommunications companies should pay an annual fee of 1 to 2 percent of revenues, and the FCC should continue its sensible policy, begun last year, of auctioning off or leasing unused frequencies, not simply giving them away" (A15).

Finally, in *Electronic Media Law and Regulation*, Kenneth Creech notes that since windfall profits generated by advertising drive the media toward monopoly, thus eliminating opportunities for entrepreneurs, a progressive tax on advertising would reverse or slow the process. In our opinion, this progressive tax should be in addition to their normal income taxes. Although such fees and taxes won't cure "toxic talk," they would also make possible the subsidizing of competitive, noncommercial broadcasting systems, thereby creating a full range of alternative voices.

If these corporate entities and their sponsors were modestly taxed in this way, the revenues could be considerable. In 1990-1991, for example, just 2% of the monies earned or spent on U.S. advertising or media conglomerates that produce information and other cultural programs would have generated about $2.4 billion. By 1995, that figure jumped to an estimated $10 to $20 billion. If that money were used to create a public telecommunications trust fund for alternative television and PBS, the nation's consumers would indeed have more *real* cultural choices.

License Producers, Directors, and Other TV Personnel

Physicians, attorneys, accountants, teachers, and other professionals cannot, citing their right to freedom of speech, deliberately deceive their clients without risking censure and loss of their licenses to practice. Since the professionals on talk shows—the producers, directors, hosts, "therapists" and counselors, and other staff—pass themselves off as "experts" and since their performances affect the lives and well-being so many more people than individual professionals do in their practices, they, too, should be licensed by federal or state agencies, required to maintain strictly defined standards of professional conduct, and held responsible for the advice they provide.

This is particularly applicable to the therapeutic experts whose authority is inherently greater than that of the host and producers and, therefore, whose actions can have even greater consequences. Of course, the penalty for deliberately selling "snake oil" to the American public should be prohibiting them from "practicing" their trade in the future.

Pressure Professional Groups

It is imperative that professional groups like the American Psychological Association and the American Medical Association enter the fray on the side of the public rather than their members, who might want to increase their own fame and financial interests. In the November 1994 issue of *Pennsylvania Psychologist Quarterly*, Michael Broder, M.D., wrote about "branching out" (16) into media psychology and how "incredibly exhilarating" his experiences had been appearing on Oprah's, Donahue's, and Geraldo's programs. He also encouraged his fellow professionals to investigate similar "opportunities." We believe that his message to his peers was most unfortunate.

Currently, the licensing of physicians and psychologists varies from state to state, and many states have no licensing procedures in place at all for clinical therapists and psychologists. Accordingly, professional organizations may be the best and most effective watchdogs of these practitioners. Government should pressure professional organizations to censure members who violate standards and protocols. One of the main targets of such censure should be the expert "therapists" who appear on the toxic-talk programs dispensing impossibly facile, socially destructive, sound-bite-length advice to severely troubled people. Whether they call their interventions "counseling," "therapy," or merely "advice," it is assumed by the audience that these individuals are acting in a professional capacity. It strains credulity to state or imply that the traditional safeguards built into the therapist/patient relationship—confidentiality, careful assessment on a case-by-case basis, professional accountability, and follow-up—apply in "show business." Indeed, the dramatic tension of these shows necessitates confrontation and the setting up of highly explosive situations in which the "guest" is thrust into a public crisis without the benefit of screening or evaluation to determine whether he or she can handle it.

The misuse and trivialization of therapy is, to say the very least, a dangerous fallout of toxic talk, an effect that threatens to undermine the profession's credibility and the audience's perceptions of therapeutic processes, as well as the welfare of the "guests" themselves. If these therapists have legitimate credentials, then they should do their work in a clinical setting, keep their advice limited to those whom they are treating and for whom they have responsibility, observe the conventional ethics and legal obligations applied in all physician/patient relationships, and abide by the primary rule that physicians and clinical psychologists are expected to live by: "First do no harm."

Regarding those talk-show "therapists" who have no real credentials beyond the fact that they dispense advice on the radio or on television, these same professional groups should inform the public of the quackery being practiced by these "experts," pressure television producers who attempt to legitimize their deceptive handiwork by insisting that they provide the credentials of these "experts," and restrict membership of those who sell out to "psychobabble" and pop psychology.

In an HBO interview aired on July 15, 1995, Phil Donahue asked, "Does middle America really want a bunch of people behind closed doors deciding what we watch?" Of course, this argument about censorship is all too familiar and all too absurd. The fact of the matter is that people behind closed doors *do* determine what we watch—namely a handful of corporate moguls and the sponsors to whom they cater. The people to whom Donahue refers here are not those monied movers and shakers, but the political and legal leaders charged with the public's welfare. Public institutions cannot operate entirely in the dark whereas corporate entities can and do. Following this chapter, we've included an appendix that lists all of the equity owners of the programs we've been discussing. How many of these people are known to the general public? How many Americans are clear about their financial stakes in toxic talk and other homogenized television products. Not very many, we suspect. In this era of unprecedented mergers, increasing deregulation, and failure on the part of Washington to apply antitrust legislation to the media and other companies, it is most critical that we become media literate now. And yet, as the people who stand to gain the most by our ignorance grow in power, how long do we have before the information that we need to become literate will not be available to us?

While this book was intended to reveal some of the social, political and economic causes, damaging effects, and manipulative players involved in the toxic-talk game, we hope that it goes beyond that narrow focus and contributes to a relatively small but growing dialogue about the contemporary media and the dangers of monopolistic control. American freedom and therefore American culture as we have known them cannot survive without a free, open, and competitive forum of art and ideas. We cannot know what is worthwhile and what worthless unless we have many options available to us. And we certainly cannot afford the further numbing and dumbing of America as we enter the brave new world of the twenty-first century.

Notes

1. The courts are now considering the constitutionality of the clause. If they treat the Internet as a print medium, it will be allowed greater leeway than it would be if deemed a television medium. The reasoning behind this distinction is that television has been regarded as "an uninvited guest" in all of our homes, and therefore it is subject to greater censorship. In addition, access to television programs is harder to control or to keep out of the hands of minors than, say, "adult" magazines. It is assumed that one must have reached a certain age of maturity to be literate enough to go out and purchase a book, newspaper, or magazine and to read it. The fact is, however, the Internet is a bit of both media, and the difficulty inherent in regulating it comes down to a question of ownership. But who owns the Internet, and who is responsible for its content? Should service providers be responsible for content, or should it be the individuals from around the world who create accessible pages? Until thorny questions like these are answered, the courts will have a difficult time ruling.

Appendix

The Corporate Players:
A Directory of Producers, Owners, and Revenue

Media power is political power, and in a government of the people, by the people, and for the people, it is critical that we all become media literate if we expect to remain free. This book looked at the deceptions and misinformation of "toxic talk," America's hottest game show. We're not saying that this kind of programming represents some kind of organized plot to keep us dumb and numb to reality, but Americans certainly should be aware of the huge economic interests that media companies have in grabbing our attention by broadcasting titillating messages regardless of their truth or social value. It is also problematical that fewer than fifty men and women, the chiefs of their corporate organizations, control more than half of the ideas, information, and entertainment reaching 220 million Americans and countless others around the globe. Ben Bagdikian is surely right to assert that "it is time for Americans to examine the institutions from which they receive their daily picture of the world "(xxxi).

Certainly, as a consuming public, we should be aware of at least some of the behind-the-scenes people and occurrences that influence our lives so profoundly. If we set out to buy a car or a computer or a major appliance, many of us do research to determine the best buy for the money. Why, then, are most of us blissfully unaware of the media operations that can potentially cost so much more than the selection of a "wrong" washing machine? Even more to the point, why are we so knowledgeable about and fascinated by the sex lives and intimate relations of the dysfunctional people highlighted on these shows and almost completely ignorant of the real players, the corporate players? How many people recognize names like Tribune's C. T. Brumback (syndicator of Geraldo and Charles Perez), King World's Roger King (Oprah and Rolonda), or Multimedia's Donald Sbarra (Phil Donahue, Sally Jessy Raphael, Jerry Springer)? One thing is certain: the public may own the airwaves, but these individuals are profiting from our property.

What follows are two listings to help the reader understand these key players—those who appear on the screen, those behind the scenes, and those in the corporate suites. The first list includes the key production personnel of the most popular shows. Also included are the names of their production companies and major syndicators, the latter followed by an asterisk (*). Part 2 lists the chief parent companies of the major owner/syndicators (i.e., those indicated by asterisks in part 1), their key personnel, and their revenues. The first list was compiled from on-screen credits at the beginning of the 1995-1996 television season, and the information in part 2 was derived from the 1995 *Standard and Poor's Register* and *Hoover's Handbook Database.*

Part 1: The Programs

Carnie (Debut: September 11, 1995)

Staff
Host: Carnie Wilson
Director: Hal Grant
Executive Producer: Cathy Chermol
Senior Producer: Andy Lassner
Supervising Pproducer: Rob Dauber

Production/Syndication
Telepictures Productions
Warner Brothers Domestic Television Distribution
Time Warner Entertainment*

The Richard Bey Show

Staff
Executive Producer: David Sittenfel
Coordinating Producer: Alexandra Cohen
Producer: Kathy Sutula

Production/Syndication
Chris-Craft Television Productions*
United Television Productions
All-American Television

Danny! (Debut: September 11, 1995)

Staff
Host: Danny Bonaduce
Executive Producer: Velma Cato
Director: Chris Darley

Production/Syndication
Faded Denim Productions, Ltd.
Buena Vista Television

Donahue

Staff
Host: Phil Donahue
Executive Producer: Patrick McMillen
Supervisory Producer: Albert Lewitinn
Director: Bryan Russo

Production/Syndication
Multimedia Entertainment*

The Gordon Elliott Show

Staff
Executive Producer: Terry Murphy
Senior Producer: Cyndi Wolfman Scott
Producer: Joanne Cerrone
Director: Brian Campbell

Production/Syndication
CBS Entertainment*

Geraldo
Staff
Host: Geraldo Rivera
Executive Producer: Jose Pretlow

Supervising Producer: Deborah J. Mitchell
Senior Producer: Kevin McMahon
Producer: Clare Hickey
Director Don McSorley

Production/Syndication
Investigative News Group (Geraldo Rivera, equity owner)
Tribune Broadcasting*

The Jenny Jones Show

Staff
Executive Producers: Debby Harwick Glavin, Ed Glavin, and
     David Salzman
Director: Tom Maguire

Production/Syndication
Telepictures Productions
Time Warner Entertainment*

Ricki Lake

Staff
Executive Producers: Garth Ancier and Gail Steinberg
Supervising Producer: Stuart Krasnow
Senior Producer: Halle Sherwin
Director: Bob McKinnon

Production/Syndication
The Garth Ancier Company
Columbia TriStar
Sony Pictures Entertainment*

Charles Perez

Staff
Executive Producer: Ray Nunn
Senior Producer: Felice Desner
Supervising Producer: Herman "Uncle Reds" Williams
Producer: Lauren Nadler
Director: Alex Tyner

Production/Syndication
Tribune Broadcasting*

Maury Povich

Staff
Executive Producer: Diane Rappoport

Production/Syndication
MoPo Productions (Maury Povich, equity owner)
Paramount Pictures Entertainment
Viacom*

Sally Jessy Raphael

Staff
Executive Producer: Maurice Tunick
Senior Producer: Amy Rosenblum
Coordinating Producer: Jill Blackstone
Producer: Holly Jacobs
Director: Kit Carson

Production/Syndication
Multimedia Entertainment*

Rolonda

Staff
Host: Rolonda Watts
Executive Producers: Michael King and Roger King
Co-Executive Producer: Marilyn Gill
Supervising Producer: Rolonda Watts
Senior Producer: Glenda Shaw
Director: Joey Ford

Production/Syndication
RWS Productions (Rolonda Watts, equity owner)
King World*

The Jerry Springer Show

Staff
Executive Producer: Richard Dominick
Senior Producer: Annette Grundy
Director: Greg Klazura

Production/Syndication
Multimedia Entertainment*

Tempestt (Debut: September 11, 1995)

Staff
Executive Producers: Dick Clark and Donna Benner Ingber
Supervision Producer: April Benimowitz
Director: Glenn Weiss

Production/Syndication
Dick Clark Productions
Columbia TriStar
Sony Pictures Entertainment*

Montel

Staff
Host: Montel Williams
Executive Producers: Montel Williams, Herman Rush, Freddie
    Fields, Mary L. Duffy
Senior Supervising Producer: Alex Williamson
Supervising Producer: Liz Frillicci
Senior Producer: Neal Kendall
Producer: Stacy Galonsky
Director Peter Kimball

Production/Syndication
Out of My Way Productions
Chris-Craft Television Productions*
United Television Productions
Viacom*

The Oprah Winfrey Show

Staff
Executive Producer: Dianne Hudson
Supervision Producer: Oprah Winfrey
Senior Producers: David Boul, Alice McGee, and Ellen Rakieten
Producer: Robe Imoriano

Production/Syndication
Harpo Productions (Oprah Winfrey, equity owner)
King World*

Gabrielle (Debut September 11, 1995)

Staff
Host: Gabrielle Carteris
Executive Producer: J. Darlene Hayes
Co-Executive Producer: Gabrielle Carteris
Supervising Producer: Edward L. Leon
Producer: Shannon O'Rourke
Director: Joe Carolei

Production/Syndication
Mont Lane Productions, Inc.
Fox Lane Productions, Inc.
Gabco Productions, Inc.
Twentieth Century Fox Film Corporation

Leeza

Staff
Host: Leeza Gibbons
Executive Producers: Nancy Alspaugh and Leeza Gibbons
Supervising Producer: Laura Gelles
Producer: David Perler
Director: Paul Forrest

Production/Syndication
Leeza Gibbons Enterprises
Paramount Pictures
Viacom*

Mark Walberg (Debut September 11, 1995)

Staff
Executive Producer: Randall Douthit
Supervising Producer: Kimberly Agle
Director: Mark Gentile

Production/Syndication
Genesis Entertainment
New World Entertainment Company

Part 2: Major Owners and Syndicators

Chris-Craft Industries, Inc
767 Fifth Avenue
New York, NY 10153
212-421-0200

Chairman and President: Herbert J. Siegel
Executive Vice President: Evan C. Thompson
1994 Revenue: $439.7 million
Programs: Richard Bey, Montel Williams

CBS Entertainment
51 West 52nd Street
New York, NY 10019
212-975-4321

Chairman, President, and CEO: Laurence A. Tisch
Vice President, CBS Broadcasting Group: Howard Stringer
Executive Vice President/President, CBS Television Network:
    Peter A. Lund
1993 Sales: $3.51 billion
Programs: Gordon Elliott

King World Productions, Inc.
1700 Broadway
New York, NY 10019
212-315-4000

Chairman: Roger King
President and CEO: Michael King
Executive Vice President and COO: Stephen W. Palley
1994 Sale: $474.3 million
Programs: Rolonda, Oprah Winfrey, Geraldo Rivera (beginning in
    1996)

Multimedia, Inc.
305 S. Main Street
Box 1688
Greenville, SC 29602
803-298-4373

Chairman and CEO: Donald D. Sbarra
President and COO: Douglas J. Greenlaw
Vice President/President, Multimedia Entertainment : Robert L.
    Turner
1994 Sales: $634.6 million
Programs: Phil Donahue, Sally Jessy Raphael, Jerry Springer

Sony Pictures Entertainment, Inc.
711 Fifth Avenue
New York, NY 10022
212-751-4400

Chairman: Akio Morita
President and CEO: Norio Ohga
President and CEO, Sony Corp. of America: Michael P. Schulhof
Co-chair and CEO, Sony Pictures: Peter Guber
Co-chair, Sony Pictures: Frank Price
1994 Sales (Sony Corp): $36.25 billion
1994 Sales (Sony Pictures Entertainment): $3.2 billion (19%)
Programs: Ricki Lake, Tempestt

Time Warner, Inc.
1271 Avenue of the Americas
New York, NY 10020
212-484-8000

Chairman, President & CEO: Gerald M. Levin
Executive Vice Presidents: Peter R. Haje, Bert W. Wasserman
Chairman, Executive Committee: J. Richard Munro
1994 Revenue: $14.54 billion
Programs: Carnie, Jenny Jones

The Tribune Company
435 N. Michigan Avenue
Chicago, IL 60611
312-222-9100

Chairman & CEO: C. T. Brumback
President & COO: John W. Madigan
Executive Vice President, Media Operations: James C. Dowdle
1994 Revenue: $1.95 billion
Programs: Charles Perez, Geraldo

Viacom, Inc.
1515 Broadway
New York, NY 10036
212-258-6000

Chairman: Sumner M. Redstone
President & CEO: Frank J. Biondi, Jr.
1994 Sales: $7.36 billion
Programs: Maury Povich, Montel Williams, Leeza Gibbons

Works Cited

Abt, Vicki. "Phil, Sally, Oprah Drag Society Down." New York *Daily News* 4 Sept. 1994: C19.

Abt, Vicki, James F. Smith, and Eugene Christiansen. *The Business of Risk: Playing the Game in Mainstream America.* Lawrence: UP of Kansas, 1985.

Abt, Vicki, and Martin McGurrin. "The Politics of Problem Gambling: Issues in the Professionalization of Addiction Counseling." *Gambling and Public Policy.* Ed. William Eadington and Judy Cornelius. Reno: U of Nevada P, 1991: 657-66.

Abt, Vicki, and Mel Seesholtz. "The Shameless World of Phil, Sally and Oprah: Television Talk Shows and the Deconstructing of Society." *Journal of Popular Culture* 28 (Summer 1994): 195-216.

Andersen, Kurt. "Pop Goes the Culture." *Time* 16 June 1986: 68-74.

Andrews, Edmund L. "Mr. Murdoch Goes to Washington: The G.O.P. Welcome Is Warm Indeed." *New York Times* 23 July 1995, sec. 3: 1.

——. "Ownership Limits a Problem? Just Change the Rules." *New York Times* 23 July 1995, sec. 3: 11.

Arendt, Hannah. *Eichmann in Jerusalem: A Report on the Banality of Evil.* Rev. ed. New York: Viking, 1977.

Auletta, Ken. *Three Blind Mice: How the TV Networks Lost Their Way.* New York: Random, 1991.

Aversa, Jeannine. "Cable TV Rates Are Rising, but Congress Is Silent." *Philadelphia Inquirer* 28 June 1996: D1, D6.

——. "Final Nod for CBS Takeover." *Philadelphia Inquirer* 23 Nov. 1995: D1, D9.

——. "Giant Radio Merger Approved." *Philadelphia Inquirer* 27 Dec. 1996: C1.

Bagdikian, Ben. *The Media Monopoly.* 4th ed. Boston: Beacon, 1992.

Baker, Russell. "How the Going Got Bad." *New York Times* 18 July 1995: A13.

Banfield, Edward. *The Unheavenly City Revisited.* Boston: Little, Brown, 1974.

Barber, Benjamin R. *Jihad vs. McWorld.* New York: Times, 1995.

181

Barnouw, Erik. *The Sponsor*. New York: Oxford UP, 1978.

Beatty, Sally Goll. "Are Daytime Shows Too Hot to Handle?" *Wall Street Journal* 2 Nov. 1995: B10.

Bellafante, Gina. "Playing 'Get the Guest.'" *Time* 27 Mar. 1995: 77.

Bellah, Robert N. et al. *The Good Society*. New York: Vintage, 1991.

Berger, Peter, and Thomas Luckmann. *The Social Construction of Reality: A Treatise in the Sociology of Knowledge*. New York: Doubleday, 1967.

"The Best of '96." *TV Guide* 4-10 Jan. 1997.

Bly, Nellie. *Oprah!: Up Close and Down Home*. New York: Zebra, 1993.

Bly, Robert. *The Sibling Society*. New York: Addison-Wesley, 1996.

Boorstin, Daniel. *The Image: A Guide to Pseudo-Events in America*. New York: Atheneum, 1961.

Bork, Robert. *Slouching Toward Gomorrah: Modern Liberalism and American Decline*. New York: HarperCollins, 1996.

Bradsher, Keith. "Talk-Show Guest Is Guilty of Second-Degree Murder." *New York Times* 13 Nov. 1996: A14.

——. "Widest Gap in Incomes? Research Points to U.S.: Study Covered Industrial Nations in the 1980's." *New York Times* 27 Oct. 1995: D2.

Broder, Michael. "Media Psychology: An Old Practice Becomes a New Specialty." *Pennsylvania Psychologist Quarterly* Nov. 1994: 16.

Burns, Elizabeth. *Theatricality: A Study of Convention in the Theatre and in Social Life*. New York: Harper, 1973.

Bushman, Richard L. "The Genteel Republic." *Wilson Quarterly* Autumn 1996: 14-23.

Caillois, Roger. *Man, Play, and Games*. Trans. Meyer Barash. New York: Schocken, 1979.

Carter, Bill. "After the Mergers: How the Networks Fit." *New York Times* 2 Aug. 1995: D1.

Carter, Kevin. "Radio Giants' Deal to Unite 6 Local Stations." *Philadelphia Inquirer* 21 June 1996: A1, A18.

Cassel, Andrew. "Media Empires Built on Myths and Imagery." *Philadelphia Inquirer* 6 Aug. 1995: D1, D5.

——. "Relaxation of Rules Makes Westinghouse-Infinity Merger Possible." *Philadelphia Inquirer* 21 June 1996: A19.

Cialdini, Robert. *Influence: How and Why People Agree to Things*. New York: Quill, 1984.

Covington, William G., Jr. "The Financial Interest and Syndication Rules in Retrospect: History and Analysis." *Communications and the Law* 16 (June 1994): 3-19.

Creech, Kenneth. *Electronic Media Law and Regulation.* Boston: Focal, 1993.

Dershowitz, Alan. *The Abuse Excuse and Other Cop-Outs, Sob Stories, and Evasions of Responsibility.* Boston: Little, Brown, 1994.

Diani, Marco, ed. *The Immaterial Society: Design, Culture and Technology in the Post-Modern World.* Englewood Cliffs: Prentice-Hall, 1992.

"Disney's World." *Newsweek* 14 Aug. 1995: 21-31.

Dominick, Joseph. *The Dynamics of Mass Communication.* 2nd ed. New York: Random/Knopf, 1987.

Donahue, Phil *The Human Animal* New York: Simon & Schuster, 1985.

Dowd, Maureen. "Talk Is Cheap." *New York Times* 26 Oct. 1995: A25.

Duggan, Ervin S. "The Twilight Zone of Kids' TV." *New York Times* 25 June 1996: A21.

Durkheim, Emile. *Suicide: A Study in Sociology.* 1897. Trans. John Spaulding and George Simpson. New York: Free, 1951.

Ehrenreich, Barbara. *Fear of Falling: The Inner Life of the Middle Class.* New York: Harper, 1990.

Fabrikant, Geraldine. "How Ted Turner Plans to Play for a Network." *New York Times* 21 Aug. 1995: D1, D6.

——. "Turner Board Won't Make Bid for King World." *New York Times* 22 Aug. 1995: D1, D6.

Fallows, James. *Breaking the News: How the Media Undermine American Democracy.* New York: Pantheon, 1996.

Fiedler, Leslie. *Tyranny of the Normal: Essays on Bioethics, Theology, and Myth.* New York: David R. Godine, 1996.

Frank, Robert, and Philip Cook. *The Winner-Take-All Society.* New York: Free, 1995.

Friend, Tad. "White Trash Nation." *New York Times* 22 Aug. 1994: 22-30.

Fussell, Paul. *BAD, or the Dumbing of America.* New York: Summit, 1991.

Galbraith, John Kenneth. *The Good Society: The Humane Agenda.* Boston: Houghton Mifflin, 1996.

Gergen, Kenneth. *The Saturated Self: Dilemmas of Identity in Contemporary Life.* New York: Basic, 1991.

184 Works Cited

Geyer, Georgie Ann. *Americans No More: The End of Citizenship*. New York: Grove/Atlantic, 1996.

Glaberson, William. "The Press: Bought and Sold and Gray All Over." *New York Times* 30 July 1995, sec. 4: 1.

Goffman, Erving. *Behavior in Public Places*. Glencoe: Free, 1963.

——. *Frame Analysis*. Cambridge: Harvard UP, 1974.

——. "Where the Action Is." *Interaction Ritual: Essays on Face-to-Face Behavior*. Garden City: Anchor, 1967.

Goldfarb, Jeffrey. *The Cynical Society: The Culture of Politics and the Politics of Culture in American Life*. Chicago: U of Chicago P, 1991.

Goodman, Walter. "Daytime TV Talk: The Issue of Class." *New York Times* 1 Nov. 1995: C15, C21.

Gray, Ellen. "Hey, It's OK! I Saw It on TV! Are These People Talking Us into Deviant Behavior." *Philadelphia Daily News* 14 July 1994: 46, 48.

Greenberg, Bradley S. et al. "The Content of Television Talk Shows: Topics, Guests and Interactions." Department of Communication, Michigan State University (report prepared by the Kaiser Family Foundation), Nov. 1995.

Griffin, Nancy, and Kim Masters. *Hit & Run: How Jon Peters and Peter Guber Took Sony for a Ride in Hollywood*. New York: Simon & Schuster, 1996.

Grimes, Tom. *City of God: A Novel*. New York: Norton, 1995.

Grimes, William "The Deconstruction on Jerry, Maury and Montel." *New York Times* 10 Dec. 1995: E7.

Grossman, Lawrence. "Cut the Public in on the Mega-Mergers." *New York Times* 21 Aug. 1995: A15.

Groves, Martha. "Summer Doldrums? Not in Entertainment Firms' Boardrooms." *Philadelphia Inquirer* 1 Sept. 1995: C1, C7.

Heaton, Jeanne, and Nona Wilson. *Tuning in Trouble: Talk TV's Destructive Impact on Mental Health*. New York: Joss-Bassey, 1995.

Herbert, Bob. "Double Exploitation." *New York Times* 26 Feb. 1996: A13.

Henry, William A., 3rd. *In Defense of Elitism*. New York: Doubleday, 1995.

Himmelfarb, Gertrude. *The Demoralization of Society: From Victorian Virtues to Modern Values*. New York: Knopf, 1995.

Holden, Stephen. "The Media Monster Lurking Within." *New York Times* 1 Oct. 1995: H15.

Holmes, Steven A. "Income Disparity Between Poorest and Richest Rises." *New York Times* 20 June 1996: A1, A18.

Hoover's Handbook Database. Austin: Reference P, 1995.

Huizinga, Johan. *Homo Ludens: A Study of the Play-Element in Culture*. 1938. Boston: Beacon, 1955.

Huston, Aletha, et al. *Big World, Small Screen: The Role of Television in American Society*. Lincoln: U of Nebraska P, 1992 (commissioned by the American Psychological Association).

Huxley, Aldous. *Brave New World*. 1932. New York: Harper Perennial, 1989.

Jacobs, A. J. "On the Wild Side: It's All in a Day of Daytime Trash at the Jerry Springer Show." *Entertainment Weekly* 12 May 1995: 34-37.

Kakutani, Michiko. "When Fluidity Replaces Maturity." *New York Times* 20 Mar. 1995: C11.

Kaminer, Wendy. *I'm Dysfunctional, You're Dysfunctional: The Recovery Movement and Other Self-Help Fashions*. Reading: Addison-Wesley, 1992.

Kanner, Bernice. "Americans Lie, or So They Say." *New York Times* 2 June 1996, Styles sec.: 43-44.

Kaplan, Janice. "Are Talk Shows Out of Control?" *TV Guide* 1 Apr. 1995: 10-15.

Kazin, Michael. *The Populist Persuasion: An American History*. New York: Basic, 1995.

Kolbert, Elizabeth. "Americans Despair of Popular Culture." *New York Times* 20 Aug. 1995, sec. 2: 1.

——. "Wages of Deceit: Untrue Confessions." *New York Times* 11 June 1995, Arts and Leisure: 1, 29.

Kovich, Bill. "Big Deals, With Journalism Thrown In." *New York Times* 3 Aug. 1995: A25.

Kozol, Jonathan. *Illiterate America*. New York: Doubleday, 1985.

Kunstler, James Howard. *The Geography of Nowhere: The Rise and Decline of America's Man-Made Landscape*. New York: Touchstone, 1993.

Kurtz, Howard. *Media Circus: The Trouble with America's Newspapers*. New York: Times, 1993.

Lacayo, Richard. "Violent Reaction: Bob Dole's Broadside Against Sex and Violence in Popular Culture Sets off a Furious Debate on Responsibility." *Time* 12 June 1995: 25-30.

Landler, Mark. "I.R.S. Ruling Clears the Way for Viacom's Cable Spin-off." *New York Times* 18 June 1996: D1.

——. "Merging Voices That Roar: Is a Radio Deal Too Big?" *New York Times* 21 June 1996: D1, D5.

——. "Now, Bell Atlantic Plans to Buy Nynex, Not Merge With It." *New York Times* 27 June 1996: D4.

——. "Viacom Makes New Cable Deal with Tele-Communications." *New York Times* 26 July 1995: D1.

Lasch, Christopher. *The Culture of Narcissism: American Life in an Age of Diminishing Expectations*. New York: Norton, 1979.

——. *The Revolt of the Elites and the Betrayal of Democracy*. New York: Norton, 1995.

"Let's Get Big: Media Merger Mania—Is the Public Served?" *New York Times* 2 Sept. 1995: 18.

Levinson, Marc. "Mickey's Wake-Up Call: Now, the Spotlight Shifts to Capitol Hill." *Newsweek* 14 Aug. 1995: 27.

Lewis, Peter H. "Judges Turn Back Law to Regulate Internet Decency." *New York Times* 13 June 1996: A1, B11.

Mander, Jerry. *Four Arguments for the Elimination of Television*. New York: Quill, 1977.

Maney, Kevin. "Media Firms Shift to Gain Product Control." *USA Today* 14 Sept. 1995: B1, B2.

Mankiewicz, Frank, and Joel Swerdlow. *Remote Control: Television and the Manipulation of American Life*. New York: Ballantine, 1978.

Matza, Michael. "In Suburbs, Safe but Not Sound." *Philadelphia Inquirer* 3 Sept. 1995: A1, A22.

Mazzocco, Dennis. *Networks of Power: Corporate TV's Threat to Democracy*. Boston: South End, 1994.

McKibben, Bill. *The Age of Missing Information*. New York: Random, 1992.

McLuhan, Marshall. *Understanding Media: The Extensions of Man*. New York: Signet, 1964.

Meredith, Robyn. "Media Deals." *USA Today* 14 Sept. 1995: B1.

Meyrowitz, Joshua. *No Sense of Place: The Impact of Electronic Media on Social Behavior*. New York: Oxford UP, 1985.

Mifflin, Lawrie. "2 Daytime Talk Shows Are Canceled." *New York Times* 3 Jan. 1996: C15.

Minow, Newton N., and Craig L. LaMay. *Abandoned in the Wasteland: Children, Television and the First Amendment*. New York: Hill & Wang, 1995.

Mitroff, Ian, and Warren Bennis. *The Unreality Industry: The Deliberate Manufacturing of Falsehood and What It Is Doing to Our Lives.* New York: Birch Lane, 1989.

Morris, James. "Democracy Beguiled." *Wilson Quarterly* Autumn 1996: 24-35.

Nissen, Todd. "Trial in Slaying of Gay Admirer Spotlights Seedy Side to TV Talk Shows." *Philadelphia Inquirer* 7 Oct. 1996: A5.

Ortega y Gasset, Jose, trans. *The Revolt of the Masses.* 1930. New York: Norton, 1932.

Parenti, Michael. *Make-Believe Media: The Politics of Entertainment.* New York: St. Martin's, 1992.

Peele, Stanton. *Diseasing of America: How We Allowed Recovery Zealots and the Treatment Industry to Convince Us We Are Out of Control.* New York: Lexington/Free, 1989.

——. *The Meaning of Addiction: Compulsive Experience and Its Interpretations.* Lexington, MA: Lexington/D.C. Heath, 1985.

Phillips, B. J. "Disney Acquires a World of Power." *Philadelphia Inquirer* 2 Aug. 1995: C1.

Postman, Neil. *Amusing Ourselves to Death: Public Discourse in the Age of Show Business.* New York: Viking, 1985.

——. *Technopoly: The Surrender of Culture to Technology.* New York: Knopf, 1992.

Postman, Neil, and Steve Powers. *How to Watch TV News.* New York: Penguin, 1992.

Rheingold, Howard. *Virtual Reality: The Revolutionary Technology of Computer-Generated Artificial Worlds and How It Promises and Threatens to Transform Business and Society.* New York: Summit, 1991.

Rich, Frank. "The Disney Trap." *New York Times* 5 Aug. 1995: A19.

——. "Down the Tube." *New York Times* 15 June 1996: A19.

——. "More Mogul Madness." *New York Times* 13 Nov. 1996: A23.

Rieff, Philip. *The Triumph of the Therapeutic: Uses of Faith After Freud.* New York: Harper, 1968.

Roberts, Johnnie L. "The Men Behind the Megadeals." *Newsweek* 14 Aug. 1995: 22-27.

Rosenthal, Raymond, ed. *McLuhan: Pro & Con.* New York: Penguin, 1969.

Rothenberg, Randall. "A Million Channels and Nothing On." *New York Times* 23 Oct. 1996: A25.

Rozansky, Michael L. "Media Deals Put Ted Turner in the Spotlight." *Philadelphia Inquirer* 6 Aug. 1995: D1, D5.

———. "Turner and Time: A Deal or a Coup." *Philadelphia Inquirer* 17 Sept. 1995: D1, D2.

Ruben, David. "New Trouble on TV." *Parenting* Oct. 1995: 21.

Sandel, Michael. *Democracy's Discontent.* Cambridge: Harvard UP, 1996.

Schickel, Richard. *Intimate Strangers: The Culture of Celebrity.* Garden City: Doubleday, 1985.

Seplow, Stephen. "Now, They're Talking about Talk Shows." *Philadelphia Inquirer* 12 Mar. 1995: A4.

———. "Seduced and Abandoned: If You Tell All on TV, Do You Find Catharsis? Or More Headaches?" *Philadelphia Inquirer Magazine* 24 Sept. 1995: 12-14, 24, 26, 26.

———. "Titans of Talk Are Pressured to Get Kinks Out of Daytime TV." *Philadelphia Inquirer* 5 Nov. 1995: A1, A19.

Shachtman, Tom. *The Inarticulate Society: Eloquence and Culture in America.* New York: Free, 1995.

Shattuck, Roger. *Forbidden Knowledge: From Prometheus to Pornography.* New York: St. Martin's, 1996.

Shister, Gail. "Geraldo Rivera Says Ratings Drop Won't Run Him off the High Road." *Philadelphia Inquirer* 22 Feb. 1996: C8.

———. "Talk Shows Must Change to Survive, Hosts Say after Murder Verdict." *Philadelphia Inquirer* 13 Nov. 1996: D8.

Slater, Philip. *The Pursuit of Loneliness: American Culture at the Breaking Point.* Boston: Beacon, 1970.

Sloan, Allan. "Cashing in Their Chips." *Newsweek* 14 Aug. 1995: 24-25.

Slobodzian, Joseph A. "Woman Sues 'Charles Perez' Over Impersonator." *Philadelphia Inquirer* 29 Sept. 1995: B1, B4.

Slouka, Mark. *War of the Worlds: Cyberspace and the High-Tech Assault on Reality.* New York: Basic, 1995.

Spector, Malcolm, and John Kitsuse. *Constructing Social Problems.* New York: Aldine, 1987.

Speers, W. "Montel Williams Accused of Sexual Harassment." *Philadelphia Inquirer* 14 June 1996: F2.

Standard & Poor's Register. New York: McGraw-Hill, 1995.

Stasio, Marilyn. "When Talk Shows Become Horror Shows." *Cosmopolitan* Oct. 1995: 250-53.

Sterngold, James. "Hollywood the Blasé Is Impressed." *New York Times* 31 Aug. 1995: D4.

Stets, Dan. "Law Experts Hail Internet Ruling as Likely to Last." *Philadelphia Inquirer* 16 June 1996: 1E.

Stoll, Clifford. *Silicon Snake Oil: Second Thoughts on the Information Highway.* New York: Doubleday, 1995.

Stone, Joseph, and Tim Yohn. *Prime Time and Misdemeanors: Investigating the 1950's TV Quiz Scandal: A DA's Account.* New Brunswick: Rutgers UP, 1992.

Stonehill, Brian. "Looking for Peace in the Culture War." *Philadelphia Inquirer* 6 July 1995: A11.

Sujo, Aly. "Va. Group Assails Disney's Character." *Philadelphia Inquirer* 3 Sept. 1995: A3.

Sykes, Charles J. *A Nation of Victims: The Decay of the American Character.* New York: St. Martin's, 1992.

Szasz, Thomas. *The Myth of Mental Illness.* New York: Hober/Harper, 1961.

Talbot, Mary. "Talk Shows on the Brain." New York *Daily News* 30 July 1995, CitySmarts: 3+.

Taylor, Gary. *Cultural Selection.* New York: Basic, 1996.

Thurow, Lester. *Head to Head: The Coming Economic Battle Among Japan, Europe, and America.* New York: Warner, 1992.

"Tribune's Tower in TV." *Broadcasting and Cable* 22 Mar. 1993: 15-17.

Turow, Joseph. "The Organizational Underpinnings of Contemporary Media Conglomerates." *Communication Research* Dec. 1992: 682-704.

Twitchell, James. "But First, a Word from Our Sponsor." *Wilson Quarterly* Summer 1996: 68-77.

Waldron, Robert. *Ricki!: The Unauthorized Biography of Ricki Lake.* New York: Boulevard, 1995.

Washburn, Katharine, and John Thornton, eds. *Dumbing Down.* New York: Norton, 1996.

Wechsler, Pat, and Roger D. Friedman. "Phil Donahue Gets the Last Laugh." *New York* 21 Aug. 1995: 11-12.

Weinraub, Bernard. "How 'To Die For' Managed to Open at Simpson Finale." *New York Times* 10 Oct. 1995: C13, C14.

Whitney, Jane. "When Talk Gets Too Cheap." *U.S. News and World Report* 12 June 1995: 57-58.

Whorf, Benjamin. *Language, Thought and Reality*. Cambridge: Technology P, 1956.

Williams, Jeannie. "News & Views: Rivera's Code of TV Conduct." *USA Today* 5 Jan. 1996: 2D.

Williams, Montel. *Mountain, Get Out of My Way*. New York: TWAB, 1995.

Wollenberg, Skip. "Time Bids for Turner Networks." *Philadelphia Inquirer* 31 Aug. 1995: C1, C8.

Zoglin, Richard. "A Company Under Fire: Targeted as the Chief Cultural Offender, Time Warner Struggles to Define Itself." *Time* 12 June 1995: 37-39.

Index

191